CARING FOR OUR COMMON HOME

CARING FOR OUR COMMON HOME

A Practical Guide to *Laudato Si'*

CATHERINE WRIGHT

Paulist Press
New York / Mahwah, NJ

The Scripture quotations contained herein are from the New Revised Standard Version: Catholic Edition, Copyright © 1989 and 1993, by the Division of Christian Education of the National Council of the Churches of Christ in the United States of America. Used by permission. All rights reserved.

"Daily Examen" sections at the end of each chapter are adapted from "How Can I Pray" at ignatianspirituality .com.

Cover image by kukuruxa/Shutterstock.com
Cover and book design by Lynn Else

Library of Congress Cataloging-in-Publication Data
Names: Wright, Catherine (Assistant Professor of Religion and Philosophy), author.
Title: Caring for our common home : a practical guide to Laudato si' / Catherine Wright.
Description: New York / Mahwah : Paulist Press, 2020. | Summary: "Living Laudato Sí connects the problems facing our common home with both the theology of Laudato Si' and concrete, hope-filled activities Christians are undertaking to mitigate our ecological crises and inspire the deep commitment to creation the gospel demands"—Provided by publisher.
Identifiers: LCCN 2019026250 (print) | LCCN 2019026251 (ebook) | ISBN 9780809154470 (paperback) | ISBN 9781587688393 (ebook)
Subjects: LCSH: Human ecology—Religious aspects—Catholic Church. | Ecotheology. | Catholic Church. Pope (2013– : Francis) Laudato si'.
Classification: LCC BX1795.H82 W75 2020 (print) | LCC BX1795.H82 (ebook) | DDC 261.8/8—dc23
LC record available at https://lccn.loc.gov/2019026250
LC ebook record available at https://lccn.loc.gov/2019026251

ISBN 978-0-8091-5447-0 (paperback)
ISBN 978-1-58768-839-3 (e-book)

Published by Paulist Press
997 Macarthur Boulevard
Mahwah, New Jersey 07430
www.paulistpress.com

Printed and bound in the
United States of America

CONTENTS

PREFACE

Overview of *Laudato Si'*

Laudato Si' will change the way you understand the great commandments to love God with every fiber of your being and to love your neighbor as yourself. *Laudato Si'* is a phrase taken from St. Francis of Assisi's Canticle of the Sun that gives praise to God for creating such an amazing world that glorifies God. It can be translated as "Praise Be to You," and captures both the wonder and awe of our earthly neighbors we have lost, and the joy and love we need to faithfully care for our common home. *Laudato Si'* is the title of the letter (called an encyclical) from Pope Francis to the world that was released on Pentecost in 2015, in which he urgently calls for *ecological conversion.* He wrote this letter because he understands the poverty so many are facing today and sees how poverty and ecological degradation go hand in hand. Pope Francis has committed to live in solidarity with those pushed to the margins of society just like St. Francis of Assisi did in the twelfth century: "My people are poor and I am one of them."[1] And just like his namesake, Pope Francis cares about Earth *and* the people inhabiting it. He wrote this letter to bring the world's attention to the fact that our planet is being destroyed, and how this impacts everyone—but the vulnerable even more. This commitment to Earth and the poor informs everything he does as pope.[2] This does not mean that his papal predecessors did not embrace the poor and Earth (paragraph 3–12 of *Laudato Si'* are a grateful recognition of their good work). However, the urgency of Earth's impending demise, which echoes in the cries of the poor, inspired Pope Francis to make this commitment more intentionally and repeatedly. He constantly teaches that to serve the poor means to protect our common home. He understands that this is how we are called to love God and our neighbors as ourselves.

Laudato Si' is a good reflection of the formation of Pope Francis. He earned a degree in chemistry and a licentiate in philosophy. Thus, he understands the scientific facts that are telling us how much Earth is struggling and some patterns of thinking that have contributed to this. He is also a Jesuit priest who has taught and served in Latin America since the 1960s and saw firsthand the connection between poverty and the destruction of the forests, water sources, and soil. He also may have read Peruvian theologian

Gustavo Gutierrez, who taught that true liberation of the poor requires freedom from oppressive social, political, and economic systems that dehumanize, and a liberation from selfishness. Pope Francis would have also been exposed to the ideas of Brazilian-born Leonardo Boff, who wrote *Cry of the Earth, Cry of the Poor*. He heard fellow priests from all over the world talk about how water scarcity, deforestation, food insecurity, air pollution, and oil spills made the suffering of so many much worse. These stories helped Pope Francis write *Laudato Si'*. He made space in his letter for so many grassroots voices, a powerful act of humility and servant leadership.[3]

This letter genuinely reflects how much Pope Francis loves God, all his planetary neighbors, and himself. Pope Francis's solidarity with the poor and Earth helps him structure his pastoral letter. He begins by reminding us that Earth is part of God's creation and she is our sister and mother. But she is also in pain because of us: "This sister now cries out to us because of the harm we have inflicted on her by our irresponsible use and abuse of the goods with which God has endowed her. We have come to see ourselves as her lords and masters, entitled to plunder her at will" (*LS* 2). Pope Francis speaks with urgency because this is both a physical and spiritual crisis. As we deplete our natural resources, destroying them with our habitual need to consume, we are also detaching ourselves from a knowing and loving God and our human neighbors. Chapter 1 gives readers "the best scientific research available today" to show them exactly what dangers Earth is facing. This is not done to paralyze readers with panic or guilt, but rather to evoke a deep spiritual conversion that will help them understand the rest of what he writes and inspire them to change. The next chapter is entitled "The Gospel of Creation" (chapter 2). Here the wisdom offered in the Judeo-Christian tradition is explored so that readers can connect creation care with their understanding and worship of God. This seems intuitive, but believers have become disconnected from creation, and thus they do not think caring for creation is important to their faith lives. Following this, *Laudato Si'* asks readers to look in the mirror. It exposes human mindsets and activities that are contributing to the degradation of Earth (chapter 3: "The Human Roots of the Ecological Crisis"). This self-examination is necessary so that we can learn to live in harmony with each other and with creation. He calls this chapter "Integral Ecology" (chapter 4) and in it, identifies principles that will foster a new way of living and loving. In chapter 5 ("Lines of Approach and Action"), he sets forth necessary lines of approach that will create sustainable living on the planet, so we can "escape the spiral of self-destruction which currently engulfs us" (*LS* 163). In the last chapter, entitled "Ecological Education and Spirituality" (chapter 6), Pope Francis suggests that if we dig deeply into the "treasure of Christian spiritual experience," we will find the reason and way to care for our common home. A rich Christian spirituality can inspire us to leave a better world for future generations where all Earth's inhabitants can thrive (*LS* 15).

Repeatedly, *Laudato Si'* heightens readers' awareness of the intimate relationship between the poor and Earth. Pope Francis weaves a powerful story that speaks to the interconnectivity of all Earth's life systems and the need for new ways to honestly talk about what "economy" and "progress" should be. He asks readers to examine how they value our common home so that the scales can fall from our eyes and we will see and love our planetary neighbors anew. This echoes in the second of two prayers he offers in *Laudato Si'*:

> The poor and the earth are crying out. O Lord, seize us with your power and light, help us to protect all life, to prepare for a better future, for the coming of your Kingdom of justice, peace, love, and beauty. Praise be to you! Amen.
>
> Pope Francis, "A Christian Prayer in Union with Creation," conclusion of *LS*

ACKNOWLEDGMENTS

I stand on the shoulders of those who have labored before me in the field of creation care and ecotheology—and I am immensely grateful. However, I would be remiss if I did not acknowledge the influence of the students and peers/coadventurers I have worked with on this labor of love. Being a transplanted ecotheologian from Canada, my work at a rural, southern U.S. university has been so special because of the many characters who graced my office and classrooms. Their lives, table fellowship, and wisdom have directed my writing: C. J. James, Trevor McKenzie, Kayla Gibson (editor extraordinaire!), Tripp Wright, Katie "turtle momma" Williams, Gabby Cabrera, Laura Hamrick, Ginger Walle, Edwin Bagley, Christy Cobb, and so many, many others. They have kept me on my toes, offered me their unique lenses to see the world, and made my spirit soar on some tough days. Thank you from the bottom of my heart.

INTRODUCTION

Pope Francis's letter *Laudato Si'* is important because it is a modern expression of God's special love for the poor and a promise of liberty to those held captive—something the prophets did centuries ago. Francis's 2018 Lenten message focused on how sin has caused the "love of many" to "grow cold" (Matt 24:12); our disregard of Earth and the poor is a sign that our love for God, each other, and ourselves has cooled. We need the light of the Christ to kindle a new fire of love in our hearts. But awakening to what is happening is just the first step of ecological conversion. The next step is asking "So what?" and then "Now what?"—and getting good answers to these questions. This book offers space to discover these answers. Readers will have a chance to interact and personally engage with what is happening in the world and what is written in *Laudato Si'*. There are no shortcuts and it will take more than a sound bite or a few study guides on this encyclical to live the lessons of love it contains. When people have opportunities to read, reflect, converse with others, and put their ideas into practice, lessons are learned more effectively. This is how this practical guide is designed. Its goal is to give individuals the chance to grow in their own ecological conversion experience and then have the confidence and tools to share their wisdom in workshops, Advent or Lenten small groups, sermons, youth retreats, and family conversations. These new dialogues will help celebrate our common origin, protect life on Earth, and build a better future for all.

Today Earth, and those associated with it, are being held captive by profit, ignorance, and apathy—and God is disappointed (*LS* 61). We need to be liberated by love. To bring the wisdom of *Laudato Si'* to life, Christians must reimagine the great commands to love in Matthew 22:37–40 and amend our broken relationships with God, creation, and ourselves. Matthew did not just state these commands to love without any other instructions. He gave a "how to": feed the hungry, give a thirsty person something to drink, clothe the naked, visit people in prison, and welcome the stranger. We love the simplicity of this commandment, but do we appreciate the depth of love it really advocates? To appease someone's thirst today means more than giving her a bottle of water. True, it is important to meet her immediate need, but the deeper meaning of Jesus's command is to love so deeply that you are driven to protect all water sources from degradation, making water bottles unnecessary. Similarly, easing someone's hunger today means more than donating (unwanted) cans of soup or highly processed and salt-laden nonperishables. Would you choose to feed the ones you love nonperishables at every meal? Does this food invite abundant life and health? Jesus's invitation to love demands the protection of the land and ways of life that empower people, families, and communities to feed themselves healthy food. This form of deep love is the heart of the saying—give a man a fish and he is not hungry for a day, but teach a man to fish and he never goes hungry—unless the environment degrades and the fish die. Then survival and liberation come from organizing or mobilizing people who care to protect Earth. It is vital that people of faith understand the breadth and depth of the love that Jesus invites us to partake in. Make no mistake, it is "tough love": loving God and our familiar and cuddly neighbors, as well as our prickly and often ferocious ones, are intertwined. But this deep love is also the way we will authentically love ourselves; if our Earth neighbors do not thrive, neither will we. However, who do we consider our neighbors?

Looking at the world through the many lenses of art and science, the imaginations of people in the pews can grow, which will foster the ecological conversion *Laudato Si'* desires. Therefore, the activities in this book are designed to cultivate well-rounded theological imaginations. When readers equip themselves with a greater awareness of the world of which they are a part and love more deeply, they will begin to ask important questions:

- Who is my neighbor now that I know that humanity has emerged from a sacred universe story that is 13.8 billion years old?
- Who is my neighbor now that I understand that the emergence of human beings was one of Earth's magnificent bursts of creativity, not unlike the moment when Earth erupted with color when flowering plants emerged?
- Who is my neighbor now that I appreciate that my body is powered by sunshine gifted to me via green, photosynthetic plant life?
- Who is my neighbor now that I know that I am intricately bound to all other species from fungi to parrots to kangaroos to bacteria?

Thoughtful scientists, artists, poets, laypeople, and religious are offering believers new ways of appreciating our world, ourselves, and the Creator, as you will see in this book. This new appreciation of Earth is transforming how Christians understand how to love God, neighbor, and self.

But how did our other-than-human neighbors (and the poor) cease to be our neighbors worthy of care? This is a big question that I tackled in my previous book,[1] but for now it is safe to say that humans have lost touch with Earth quite literally and have fallen out of love with creation. You cannot love what or whom you do not know. Being estranged from the natural world has led us to devalue and neglect so many of our former neighbors. Even worse, when Earth stopped being our mother and a subject of our love and affection, she became an "it"—an object or dead machine—and it became virtuous to exploit "it" to aid human development. Sadly, this dysfunctional way of being became identified with God's will. Falling out of love with Earth did not happen overnight, but the false idea of us being separate from and masters of creation still captivates so many with devastating results.

All is not lost, however. Many artists and scientists are trying to encourage us all to fall in love again. For example, Earth's many webs of life are beautifully described by German biologist Ernst Haeckel, American poet Ralph Waldo Emerson, Canadian artist Emily Carr, author Farley Mowat, and American biologist Lynne Margulis. Others such as American ecologist Rachel Carson, farmer/activist Wendell Berry, and passionate priest Thomas Berry warned us of our misuse of Earth and the immense cost of industrialization. Others still, such as Martin Luther King Jr., Leonardo Boff, Rosemary Radford Ruether, and Wangari Maathai, have taught us that social, economic, and ecological injustices are all connected and stem from our neglect of the great command to love abundantly.

All of Earth's inhabitants are our neighbors, and our personal well-being is linked with theirs. We are not separate from the ecosystems where we live and love—no matter how much we want this to be true. God is a divine family of love and St. Augustine articulated this truth about the Triune God beautifully: Lover, Beloved, Love. All that is created by God resonates with this truth, although partially. Humanity has been born into a dynamic world with a special gift: we can know and tell the long, beautiful creation story and celebrate all its many cosmic characters. Cosmic history is the greatest love story because the author of this story is infinitely abundant Love. Our vocation is to love as God loves—to the best of our abilities. When we forget we are a planetary family and are stingy with our love, we have failed to love our Creator. We also lose sight of who we are and who our neighbors are. We become apathetic to injustice and are not inspired to help God liberate those held captive. But we can love more deeply and more broadly—that is our vocation. Pope Francis asks readers to seriously ponder, "What kind of world do we want to leave those who come after us, to children who are now growing up?" (*LS* 160). If we do not imagine a better world, we will never work to make it happen. *Caring for Our Common Home: A Practical Guide to* Laudato Si' is a way of living the encyclical. It desires to move readers from comfortably knowing about *Laudato Si'* to courageously living out the many ways to love described in its pages.

One unique facet of this book is its impetus for readers to be actively engaged in the ecological conversion process. Each chapter includes sidebars that will enable you to take a breath and reflect a little more deeply on the ideas that you have read—through Scripture, art, reflections, videos, and more. This interaction will facilitate what Erin Lothes Biviano calls "holy noticing." Holy noticing is when we pay attention to Earth and, in our blossoming awareness, we appreciate how creation is indeed very good.[2] This book will offer time and space for a reader, small group, workshop, training session, or youth group to become skilled at noticing details of the world we live in and God's presence and activity in our world. This may ask you to move beyond your comfort zone into the scientific or artistic realms, but it is the necessary first step toward being in solidarity with creation. Stephen Scharper uses a quote from Gustavo Gutierrez, "Unless you know the names of poor people, you are not in solidarity with them," to explain the solidarity we ought to have with our planetary neighbors: "Unless you know the names of certain species, learn how to communicate with them, spend time with ecosystems, with rivers, discern the patterns of animals that move across your life course, your ravines, you are not in solidarity."[3] You cannot love whom you do not know, nor will you care enough to change human activities and habits that are hurting Earth.

This text is divided into four sections based on the four classic elements: water, earth, air, and fire. Within these sections, there are three chapters: an overview of what is wrong in the world, wisdom from *Laudato Si'* to help address the problems, and a brief look at the practical actions being taken to care for our common home.

In the first section, on water, the problems and impacts of water illiteracy and water poverty are examined. The next chapter lets readers explore God, Creator and Jesus, Living Water as it is presented in *Laudato Si'* to address the serious spiritual dimensions of water poverty. The final chapter will show how believers are loving their water-dwelling neighbors and themselves more deeply.

The second section is constructed in the same way but is oriented toward *terra firma*: Earth. It begins by examining Earth's landscapes and the harm being done by the way we are growing food. It will also explore the issues of food insecurity, loss of biodiversity, and extinction. The following chapter offers a portrait of the incarnation, the earthy and risen Jesus, to help address the problems facing Earth. The final chapter gives examples of how people and groups are living *Laudato Si'* by caring for our planet's sacred soil.

The focus of the third section is an exploration of Earth's atmosphere: air. The main problem to be explored is air pollution and its impact on our winged neighbors. A loss of creativity in our world is also offered as a serious problem. This will be followed in the next two chapters by a holy noticing of the Spirit in *Laudato Si'* and the positive impact being made by congregations and individuals who embrace a vibrant ecospirituality.

The last section of this book concerns fire as energy. To begin, the consequences of our addiction to fossil fuels are explored. This is followed by an outline of *Laudato Si'*s portrayal of the Trinity as creative, energetic relations of love. As with the previous sections, the final chapter will outline how the triune family has inspired prophetic energy stewardship.

This book is not the definitive "how to" for living *Laudato Si'*. Loving God, our neighbors, and ourselves is a creative enterprise that can be done in many ways. Be unafraid to walk the well-worn paths of our Christians predecessors who brought the love of the gospel to life in their own time. But remember, they never faced what we are challenged with. Our path will move into unexplored territory, but have faith that God is with us and that our labor will be the signposts for those who follow.

I

Water

INTRODUCTION

At the dawn of the twentieth century, French composer Claude Debussy gave voice to our fascination with the many moods of the sea in his symphony *La Mer*. Fifty years later, marine biologist Rachel Carson, a lover and protector of the ocean, told the story of the lure of the sea captured by Debussy in a way that echoed her scientific training:

> What is this sea, and wherein lies its power so greatly to stir the minds of men? What is the mystery of it, intangible, yet inseparably its own?...For hundreds of millions of years, all life was sea life, developing in prodigious abundance and variety....But we as man [*sic*] carry the sea's salt in our blood, and the trace of our marine heritage in our bodies, and perhaps something akin to a racial memory of that dim past lies within us....And surely the sense of these things was in Debussy's mind when he composed *La Mer*...capturing in immortal music the shining beauty, the awful power, and the eternal mystery of the sea.[1]

Our captivation with water was reinvigorated when we saw for the first time that we live on a shimmering "Blue Marble." This picture, taken from space in 1970, showed us how political borders and cultural boundaries are artificial and arbitrary. Our planet's blue lifeblood ebbs and flows, connecting everything. Water constantly circulates in and between all bodies, uniting and connecting them through time and space in a grace-filled way. The story of our watery interconnectivity needs to inform all aspects of human ecologies: education, politics, healthcare, economics, and religion.[2] Water in all its complexity should be noticed, celebrated, and respected in all human activities, including Christian catechesis, spirituality, rituals, and practice—but this is not the case. *Laudato Si'* invites humanity to recapture our lost wonder and awe of our sacred watery world and our neighbors that dwell there. Otherwise, we will not care enough to do what it takes to care for this part of creation.

Listen to the ebb and flow of Garth Stevenson's composition "On Southern Seas." This piece was the fruit of his journey to Antarctica, where his new neighbors, seals and penguins, icebergs, and other artists (garthstevenson.com) inspired him. How could this music inspire how you envision God and our watery world that God created?

In the United States we lead an extremely "wet" existence without really knowing it. Everything we do is a function of water. Even the brain with which you understand these words is 73 percent water. It might be invisible to us now, but before the industrial era, water controlled the rhythm of human activity. Water shaped where and how we lived, worked, and worshiped. The first Christian communities were defined by the desert and were dependent on clean water sources like the Jordan River. Jesus's first disciples were fishermen and spent their lives appreciating the shining beauty, devastating power, and unpredictable stinginess or generosity of the sea. We have forgotten this about water because we have been able to insulate ourselves from the fact that water is life-giving and limited. The seemingly eternal presence of water in our taps has let us take water for granted and this has seeped into our faith lives. We do not notice water, and this has hidden parts of God's message to us and diminished our understanding of the sacraments intimately linked to water.

Environmentalist David Orr observed that in our education system "ecology is unimportant for history, politics, economy, society" and as a result, we are forming "ecological yahoos" who envision Earth as a commodity with no natural or moral limits.[3] Pope Francis agrees: "[Sister, Mother Earth] now cries out to us because of the harm we have inflicted on her by our irresponsible use and abuse of the goods with which God has endowed her. We have to come to see ourselves as her lords and masters, entitled to plunder her at will" (*LS* 2). Pope Francis names a reason for our bad behavior: our technology-powered human-centeredness. This self-centeredness has led us to believe that humans are radically independent of Earth (*LS* 115). This false belief has cultivated apathy, and sometimes contempt, for our planetary neighbors and has distorted the call to love.

Chapter 1

TURBULENT TIMES

What Is Happening from Sea to Shining Sea?

A consequence of our human-centered tunnel vision is that we know very little about water, and therefore, the way we act reflects a false belief that water is infinitely abundant and incorruptible.[1] We are in for a rude awakening; the age where water is abundant, safe, and cheap is over, but we cannot live without water. Thus, those who can pay will have access to safe water while the poor will be denied access to clean water and life itself. This is not the world we want, says *Laudato Si'*:

> Even as the quality of available water is constantly diminishing, in some places there is a growing tendency, despite its scarcity, to privatize this resource, turning it into a commodity subject to the laws of the market. Yet *access to safe drinkable water is a basic and universal human right, since it is essential to human survival and, as such, is a condition for the exercise of other human rights.* Our world has a grave social debt towards the poor who lack access to drinking water, because *they are denied the right to a life consistent with their inalienable dignity.* (*LS* 30)

The social debt the world has—including Christians—can only be paid if we appreciate what water is, how it works, and why it is important to our lives and faith. Believers must intentionally become water literate so they can relearn how to be in solidarity with the Earth and the poor—and see God's presence in these activities. An authentic relationship with living water provokes the sense of wonder and awe captured by Debussy. However, people who truly love Earth's watery depths will be outraged at water poverty and act to stop this injustice.

WATER POVERTY

In the first chapter of *Laudato Si'*, water has its own subsection, and Pope Francis calls the condition of not having access to clean water *water poverty*. This is because it is a violation of the dignity of a human being (*LS* 27–30).

> The Lack of Access to Clean Water: Watch Dr. Christiana Peppard outline the problem of water scarcity at https://ed.ted.com/lessons/fresh-water-scarcity-an-introduction-to-the-problem-christiana-z-peppard. Engage the "Think" section of the video after viewing. Perhaps during your preparation for Lent or Advent, create a journal and explore the additional resources provided. With each entry, document your search through Scripture for where and when water is used and meditate on its meaning in your life.

This term, *water poverty*, reflects both the physical and spiritual dimensions of the water crisis. It also connects ecological problems with the scriptural mandate to care for the poor. The term calls Christians to act in very practical ways: increase funding to clean water projects; stop commodifying and privatizing water; educate against the wasting of water. Pope Francis is clear that this social debt is to be shouldered by everyone and not just CEOs, political leaders, or financial decision makers (*LS* 30–31). But to do this, readers must make watery ecosystems less invisible in their lives and learn how they are polluting Earth's waters and disrupting Earth's aquatic cycles.

The Energy-Food-Water Web

Life is not possible without water, so we should be very aware of how much drinkable water is available. Be sure to take the "What Do You Know about Water?" quiz in the discussion section and see how well you know water. Did it surprise you that only 2.5 percent of all the water on Earth is drinkable (i.e., freshwater), and of that water, only 0.3 percent is both accessible and drinkable (e.g., not locked away in ice or underground)? Drinkable water is quite limited, so it is urgent that we use this resource wisely. Try to imagine the top three ways humans use water. Did you guess energy production, irrigation of agriculture, and public use (water used in our homes to drink or for sanitation and landscape watering)—in that order? Creating energy to power our lifestyles uses about 45 percent of the available freshwater per day, so the more electricity we need to power our "stuff," the less water will be available for people and ecosystems. Irrigation of crops, pastures, parks, and golf courses requires the next highest amount of water—about 32 percent[2]—while water for public use is a distant third, using about 12 percent of available freshwater.[3] Is this just? The answer comes only after some holy noticing.

In the United States, approximately 89 percent of the energy produced in power plants is generated by thermoelectric systems that require water to cool steam-driven generators. As water absorbs the heat, it evaporates and is not immediately available for other uses like quenching thirst. Also, returning the warmed water to the rivers changes the temperature of the ecosystem, killing plants and fish. Since so much precious water is used to create energy, are we careful in our energy use? Unfortunately, no. In 2010 the Lawrence Livermore National Laboratory and the U.S. Department of Energy (DOE) showed that 58 percent of the total energy produced in the United States is wasted due to inefficiencies. Consumers are constantly being asked to conserve energy, but the main reason for this invitation to use less energy is to save money, not to save Earth.[4] *Laudato Si'* is clear that there are grave spiritual consequences when the wants and expectations of those living a highly technological life prohibit others from having enough water to live. Therefore, conserving energy and diminishing our dependence on unsustainable energy sources can be a great act of loving one's neighbor.

Water's connection to food is also often invisible. How much water do you think it takes to make a meal that consists of three steaks (1 kg), four large cucumber and lettuce salads (1 kg), four super chocolaty desserts (1 kg of chocolate), and one glass of wine, beer, and milk, respectively? Surprisingly, it is approximately 8,886.8 gallons (33,640 liters).[5] Exploring the hidden water footprint of the foods we eat and giving thanks for the water we use could be a faithful part of grace before meals. When we understand how much water it takes to eat the foods we love, this can motivate us to fix the problem of food waste. Americans generated about 258 million tons of material solid wastes in 2014,[6] and almost a quarter of this was food[7]—a staggering 29.4 million tons of food waste. This also means a lot of water was wasted. Imperfect Produce, a company addressing U.S. food waste, indicated that not only have they saved 9.3 million pounds of food from landfills to date, they also saved 462 million gallons of water.[8] *Laudato Si'* clearly teaches that changing both our unreasonable demand for fruits and vegetables that look "perfect" and our throwaway culture is the task given to us all by the gospel. Every dollar you spend is a value statement, and when we throw away perfectly good produce and other foods, we are contributing to water poverty.[9] Thus, parish and household shopping and eating habits can be a grace-filled way of loving God, our neighbors, and ourselves.

Public use of water in our homes and businesses is the third highest area of water consumption. Unfortunately, nationwide nearly 900 billion gallons of drinkable water are wasted annually due to leaky pipes, and poorly maintained landscape irrigation systems can waste up to 25,000 gallons of water annually.[10] Something seemingly so insignificant as turning off the tap while brushing your teeth or shaving can save nearly 5,700 gallons per year per person. Making these changes is a sign of the ecological conversion called for in *Laudato Si'*.

Water Pollution

Water pollution is another dimension of water poverty because only *clean* water will sustain life. Some are familiar with the ongoing problem of coal ash pollution in the United States and other parts of the world. Coal ash is produced by burning coal in thermoelectric power plants, and since these power plants are situated close to waterways (to draw water in for cooling), any leaks of coal ash will make the nearby water undrinkable. In North Carolina, many coal ash ponds are located close to the Catawba River, a major source of drinking water, and the intensity of Hurricane Florence raised serious concerns about water contamination. Other ways of creating energy are not much cleaner: crude oil operations that give us plastic and gas products use pipelines that often leak. One such example is the Keystone Pipeline that stretches from Alberta, Canada, to Texas. It has leaked several times and has polluted landscapes and groundwater.[11] Fracking operations that extract natural gas from deep underground are no better; the act of fracking (injecting a toxic cocktail of materials into the ground to force the gas out) and noxious byproduct wastewater ponds pose serious hazards and pollute clean water sources.

Another form of water pollution is all our plastic "stuff." When you look up the "great garbage patch" in the Pacific Ocean or the sea of plastic in the Caribbean (see photos by Carolina Power)[12] you realize that there is no "away" when we discard 8 million metric tons of plastic annually. Our disposable lifestyles are disrupting the lives of our water-dwelling and human neighbors.[13] A less visible source of plastic pollution is microplastics—plastic pieces in the water that are too small for the naked eye to see. Microplastics account for up to 8 million tons of pollution in our water systems. Some are the abrasive plastic pieces in our toothpaste and face scrubs that help brighten our teeth and skin, and small globs of paint residue rinsed down the drain.[14] We are also beginning to realize the impact of what we wear on water poverty. A new report from the Ellen MacArthur Foundation indicates that as much as 60 percent of our clothes are made from plastic, so when we wash them, tiny plastic fibers wash down the drain into rivers and oceans—and eventually into our taps and food.[15] It is astounding that one single fleece jacket can shed up to 1,900 fibers[16] and these microfibers are then ingested by fish that we then eat.[17] This certainly puts a new spin on shopping and the saying "you are what you eat." People of faith must awaken to the connections between food, water, and energy to care for our common home.

Watch the video on STRAW (Students and Teachers Restoring a Watershed) at https://vimeo.com/163463368. How did restoring a watershed restore a human community? What important factors or approaches made this a successful program? How can you connect this with other forms of justice work happening in your home, school, or church?

Another less familiar pollution source is floating dirt particles called sediment. When one inch of rain falls on one acre of forest, there is relatively little immediate runoff into local streams because it soaks into the ground and into tree roots. But a one-acre paved parking lot causes twenty thousand gallons of water to immediately flow into creeks, rivers, and lakes. This pulls enormous amounts of dirt from the banks into the water.[18] Building more and more communities and shopping centers increases the number of hard surfaces (houses, concrete, pavement) and thus, sediment pollution. This floating dirt causes many problems: the gills of fish and frogs get plugged, causing disease. Cloudy water blocks the sun, which prevents plant growth, and the destruction of stream banks disrupts natural habitats and destroys food chains. Humans also feel the effects of this pollution: soil particles clog water filtration systems, which are pricey to fix, and tourists find cloudy water very unappealing.[19] Worse, storm water runoff picks up plastic garbage, chemicals, and any wastes that overflow from industrial cattle, hog, and poultry farms—depositing it straight into the water people drink. Runoff from animal farms is a growing concern, especially in states such as Iowa where the hogs and pigs (21.8 million) far outnumber the human residents (3.14 million).[20] Thus, the call of *Laudato Si'* for access to safe, drinkable water invites many changes in our daily lives.

Disrupting Earth's Water Systems

Pope Francis repeats a truth that scientists from all over the world have discovered: Earth's natural life systems and climate patterns are being disrupted thanks to human activities. Humans have increased the amount of greenhouse gases in our atmosphere and this has led to (on average) the warming of Earth and the intensification of weather events. This hurts our sea-dwelling neighbors because oceans absorb a great amount of this heat. Sea levels have also risen due to ice melting at the poles, and there is less oxygen in the water for fish to breathe because of the warmer water. Warming oceans also have the perfect conditions for toxic algae and bacteria to grow exponentially, causing red tide and algae blooms. This is killing many of our neighbors in the world's oceans (*LS* 40).

A barometer for ocean health is our coral reefs. Due to higher acidity in the water, they have been dying. This is described as coral bleaching. Pope Francis noticed, "Who turned the wonderworld of the seas into underwater cemeteries bereft of color and life?" (*LS* 41). The survival of the coral reefs is important for several reasons. First, we have no right to deny life to these beautiful subjects of God's affection because of our fossil fuel addiction (*LS* 33). Second, scientists have found that not only are corals the backbone of a healthy ocean, they also predict the health of human communities.[21] So when we love our sea-dwelling neighbors, we are loving the Creator of such beauty—and ourselves.

In addition to changes in water chemistry, human communities are also vulnerable to changes in sea levels. When they rise due to changes in climate, coastal communities are at risk for flooding. In addition, since most land is owned privately, fishing villages cannot pick up and move to follow the cod and haddock populations that are migrating farther north to avoid warming waters. Whole communities can lose their livelihoods and culture when Earth's climate changes.

> Meditate on Gen 1:20–21, Ps 24:1–2, John 21:1–14, and Matt 4:18–19. Then listen to the stories of the first U.S. climate refugees (https://www.youtube.com/watch?v=yGiiPw29UEQ) and to North Carolina fisherman Willy Phillips (https://vimeo.com/143675329). How does Scripture speak to these dimensions of water poverty? What new attitudes or behaviors are you led to?

Laudato Si' notices and names our current state of water poverty so this reality can inform how we are living and ensure that "others will not be denied the right to a life consistent with their inalienable dignity" (*LS* 30). Water wastefulness, ignorance, indifference, and abuse makes the suffering of the poor worse because they cannot insulate themselves from rising energy and food costs, polluted drinking water, or the increasing frequency of severe weather events. The widely publicized contamination of public drinking water in Flint, Michigan, exposes the harsh reality of water poverty and injustice. A 2017 Michigan Civil Rights Commission Report found that racism and biases led to this injustice—they claim that it would not have happened in primarily white communities.[22] If Catholic Social Teaching (CST) does not address this injustice, it is lacking—but *Laudato Si'* shows that CST is very much up to the task.

Chapter 2

WISDOM FROM *LAUDATO SI'* TO GUIDE US

My soul thirsts for God,
for the living God.

Psalm 42:2

The universe unfolds in God, who fills it completely. Hence, there is a mystical meaning to be found in a leaf, in a mountain trail, in a dewdrop, in a poor person's face.

Pope Francis, *Laudato Si'*, no. 233

Laudato Si' teaches readers that God is our Creator and Jesus Christ is Living Water. Both will be explored in this chapter.

GOD, CREATOR

For Pope Francis, God is all-powerful and eternally steadfast, and God expresses this through creativity and empowerment (*LS* 77). This echoes Wisdom literature: creation exists because the Lord of the universe desired an intimate and personal relationship with all of creation and loved all that is into being (Wis 11:24). Love is the origin of all things and is the thread that binds everything together. Love was present at the birth of our universe, the moment Earth erupted with colorful plants, when human beings graced Earth; and love will continue to be present until the end times, when the cosmos rests again in God's perfect loving embrace (*LS* 117). God's love is steadfast, abundant, and life-giving: "He made streams come out of the rock and caused waters to flow down like rivers" (Ps 78:16). The Scriptures also use the destructive power of water to describe the depth of God's love: "The waters covered their adversaries; not one of them was left"

(Ps 106:11). Pope Francis reminds readers of God's love, quoting Dante Alighieri—"The love moved which moves the sun and stars" (*LS* 77). God loves creation and shows this love through the movement of the sun, moon, and stars. So, "even the fleeting life of the least of beings"—from the marine bacteria known as sea dust to the majestic loggerhead turtles—"is the object of [God's] love." In its few seconds or decades of existence, "God enfolds it with his affection" (*LS* 77). This echoes God's love for the cosmos articulated in the very opening chapter of Genesis: "God saw everything that he had made, and indeed, it was very good" (Gen 1:31). God's love and goodness infused creation with inherent dignity and worth. The watery depths bursting with life possess intrinsic worth beyond just the significance of fish or clams for human dinner plates. This does not mean that we are loved less just because God loves the American eel. Rather, we are being taught that God's love does not diminish if it is shared. We are loved, but so are they: "The entire material universe speaks of God's love, [God's] boundless affection *for us*" (*LS* 84; my italics).

Caring for creation begins by holy noticing the intrinsic worth of creation. Our distorted belief that we must be better than our other planetary neighbors and have control over them is a rejection of the sacredness of creation. Also, those who are deeply connected to Earth and remind us of the earthy cycles of life and death (e.g., indigenous peoples, the elderly, the poor, the unborn, people with disabilities, and the sick) are considered less-than-human, stripped of dignity and worth, and pushed to the margins, out of sight. Thus, healing our relationship with creation will heal and renew our human family. Pope Francis agrees: "There can be no ecology without an adequate anthropology" and vice versa (*LS* 118). God, who loves abundantly, models how we are to care for all our puzzling, prickly, and unfamiliar neighbors. This will help us know and love ourselves better: "Our openness to others, each of whom is a 'thou' capable of knowing, loving and entering into dialogue, remains the source of our nobility as human persons" (*LS* 119). Humanity is made in the image and likeness of a God who is characterized by love, creativity, empowerment, and relationality. This Creator and living God can be encountered (albeit partially) in the webs of life on this planet and in Earth's own creativity. But when we contaminate and abuse Earth's water systems, we obscure God's message of love to us and narrow our understanding of our Creator and sustainer.

Meditate on *Laudato Si'* 76, 85, and 88. How do the following worship songs espouse the truths in *Laudato Si'*? "Oceans (Where Feet May Fail)" by Hillsong UNITED at https://www.youtube.com/watch?v=dy9nwe9_xzw; "All the Ends of the Earth" by Bob Dufford, SJ, at https://www.youtube.com/watch?v=TK6gY1tkJAw. How would these songs be distorted if water is polluted and not life-giving?

When our understanding of God reflects truths from Scripture and creation, including Earth's hydrosphere, our faith will be stronger and we will want to change the way we act. We are being instructed not to destroy the home and lives of creatures of the deep nor deny water to our human brothers and sisters. Pope Francis is clear that in the Bible, there is no room for cruel human centeredness or apathy toward our neighbors on this earth. Psalm 104 reminds us that all living beings are valued by God because "by their mere existence they bless him and give him glory" (*LS* 69). Also, "the laws found in the Bible dwell on relationships, not only among individuals, but also with other living beings....Clearly, the Bible has no place for tyrannical anthropocentrism unconcerned for other creatures" (*LS* 68). A renewed love of creation will inspire right relationships with our Creator, each other, and our watery home.

JESUS, LIVING WATER

> On the last day of the festival, the great day, while Jesus was standing there, he cried out, "Let anyone who is thirsty come to me, and let the one who believes in me drink. As the scripture has said, 'Out of the believer's heart shall flow rivers of living water.'" (John 7:37–38)

> These mountains are what my Beloved is to me. Lonely valleys are quiet, pleasant, cool, shady, and flowing with fresh water. (John of the Cross, quoted in *LS* 234)

In this encyclical we are taught that Earth's waters can reveal our life-giving and life-sustaining Creator God. But we also learn much of Jesus. In the Hebrew Scriptures, God is a wellspring of life and salvation, and in Matthew 3:13–17 and John 4:7–14, Jesus is revealed to be this wellspring of living water that brings well-being and salvation. *Laudato Si'* echoes this: "From the beginning of the world, but particularly through the incarnation, the mystery of Christ is at work in a hidden manner in the natural world as a whole, without thereby impinging on its autonomy" (*LS* 99). In the next chapter we will delve deeply into Earth's landscapes and the incarnation, but here it is important to reflect on Jesus as living water, who "entered into the created cosmos, throwing in his lot with it, even to the cross" (*LS* 99). In the following passage, practice your holy noticing. Listen closely to what is being revealed about Jesus through water.

When most people read or hear John 4:7–14, they focus on a few specific things, but what about the role water plays in this story?

In this brief interaction between the Samaritan woman and Jesus, water plays a vital role. In fact, it is the reason the two begin talking. They are at a well (a source of water) and Jesus's opening line is "Give me a drink." When the conversation continues, Jesus indicates that he has "living water." At first, the woman misunderstands this to mean "flowing water" instead of the still water that would have come from a well. But the water Jesus has is "living water," and if one drinks of it one will never be thirsty again. By using this analogy, Jesus is suggesting that he himself *is* the living water. Jesus wants the woman to believe in him so that she will have eternal life. And, after some theological debate, she believes. She drinks the living water, which is Jesus as the Messiah. What if we take these verses seriously? What if Jesus is truly the living water? How differently would we then engage with water in our daily lives? What if we imagine that every single time we treat the earth as disposable we are also treating Christ as disposable?

In this story, the Samaritan woman contemplates Jesus's words and his own identification with the living water. She chooses to believe. Then, she chooses to act. May we all embrace a similar faith and action of the Samaritan woman. May we all work to preserve the Living Water.

(Dr. Christy Cobb, assistant professor of religion, Wingate University. Excerpt from a Lyceum address, fall of 2017)

Christians encountering Jesus today can learn from the Samaritan woman: our phones may give us data about water, but we need her wisdom to see that water makes our physical, social, and spiritual lives possible. By embracing Jesus as living water, we can see anew the sacred revelation communicated in Earth's watery depths. If water is no longer life-giving or if it is only something to buy and sell, then our understanding of Christ is diminished. We will also realize that we are valuable parts of Earth's sacred communion and are entrusted with the task of imagining new ways to address water poverty. Our vocation as followers of Christ means restoring dignity to the marginalized and protecting our common home (*LS* 139, 140).

Human centeredness has caused us to think of Earth as just dead space, a pleasing backdrop, or a limitless store. Holy noticing that our planet is a sacred gift allows nature to have meaning and worth outside its usefulness to humans. When we forget this giftedness, we miss how water can reflect the Gospel's message of God's liberating love. Awakening to how much God loves creation will spark powerful reactions to water poverty and cultivate a deeper hospitality toward our human neighbors (*LS* 160). If Christians courageously wade into troubled waters and reexamine how they relate to the world and the Creator of this sacred cosmos, they will drink deeply of living water.

Chapter 3

LIVING *LAUDATO SI'*

How to Care for Our Neighbors Dwelling in the Deep

Laudato Si' offers many approaches to address water poverty that would also apply to other challenges being discussed in the earth, air, and fire sections:

- Create a dialogue with many stakeholders (*LS* 139, 201)
- Cultivate a holy noticing of our common origin, mutual belonging, and shared future (*LS* 202)
- Promote ecological conversion and a change of heart (*LS* 217, 218)
- Restore ecological equilibrium and social common good as a road to inner peace (*LS* 225)
- Engage nature differently through our sacramental life (*LS* 235)

Water scarcity and poverty stems from human activities and thus we can fix this problem by making changes to the way we act. This section will offer a brief portrait of how people of faith are bringing *Laudato Si'* to life by addressing water scarcity. This will whet readers' appetites for the interactive activities, reflections, and discussion questions at the end of this section on water.

Holy noticing is the "recognition that the world is God's loving gift" (*LS* 220), including water. Water, therefore, is a medium for divine revelation.[1] Pope Francis is clear that this truth must be taught: "All Christian communities have an important role to play in ecological education. It is my hope that our seminaries and houses of formation will provide an education in responsible simplicity of life, in grateful contemplation of God's world, and in concern for the needs of the poor and the protection of the environment" (*LS* 214). Each of these aspects—responsible simplicity, grateful contemplation, concern for the poor and Earth—need to be intentionally, wisely, and prayerfully connected so that it is noticed by believers every time they reach for a glass of water, sing hymns at Mass, watch the sunrise over the water, read the bulletin, go shopping, baptize their child, reflect on a homily, or meditate on feast days—such as that of the Baptism of the Lord; Andrew the Apostle, patron of fishermen; or Arnold of Soissons, patron of brewers. The more we see water as a sacred gift and love our aquatic neighbors as ourselves, the more we will be inspired to protect our common home (*LS* 15).

Learning about water is not be enough if we do not also fall in love with our sacred "Blue Marble" and care enough to make changes. There are so many things, big and small, that believers can do to show our love of water and of our neighbors that dwell in it. An interfaith organization called Green Faith has spent the last twenty years being a great resource for holy noticers.[2] On its website are many ideas for parishes and individuals. Its starter kit offers three simple beginning steps: lower your thermostat by one degree, make your lunch or dinner vegetarian, and for one hour turn away from electronics and toward creation. All three have an impact on our water-dwelling neighbors. Fewer carbon emissions will help diminish ocean warming, rising sea levels, and acidification. Eating less meat translates into less water being used, and time away from electronics means less energy use and an improvement in our relationships with people and places. These actions help us value the intrinsic worth of creation.

Christians also need to hear examples of water stewardship from the pulpit and see it in how their parishes operate and shop. Prophetic acts of water stewardship we can do include riding our bike rather than driving, shopping locally and wisely, taking shorter showers, funding energy audits, avoiding toothpaste with microplastics, cooking family meals from scratch, promoting BYOMug meetings, dreaming up new sustainable fabrics and dyes (like Natsai Audrey Chieza did),[3] doing full loads of laundry, and hosting unplugged game nights. These are acts of Christian hospitality—just as faithful as more formal mission trips focusing on water projects in other parts of the world.[4] *Laudato Si'* invites Christian churches to embrace a balance of missions abroad and reverse missions to evangelize believers in North America.[5]

Finally, people of faith must remember that promoting ecological health can never be untangled from human well-being and justice. Many Catholic congregations, leadership conferences, and organizations have heard the cries of both the poor and creation and have responded. On December 10, 2017, the Federation of the Sisters of St. Joseph of Canada made a public commitment to water justice by becoming a "blue community."[6] They are the first group of religious in Canada to be so designated, due to their advocacy of the right of all people to safe drinking water. These nuns are water stewards in prayerful and practical ways—as their "green" Motherhouse in Toronto demonstrates. This religious congregation chose to invest in rain barrels, geothermal heating and cooling, a green roof, and permeable pavers in the parking lot that diminish storm runoff to conserve water and energy. Sister Margaret Myatt explains that this building "is part of the nuns' charism...to care for our wounded Earth" and alleviate water poverty for marginalized human populations.[7]

Watch the video made by the Sisters of St. Joseph (2018) and meditate on the wisdom in their practical and prophetic witness: https://www.youtube.com/watch?v=154KEMJplKg. How do they motivate you to care for our common home?

In the United States, prior to the 2016 elections, Bishop Paul Sirba of the diocese of Duluth, Minnesota, prepared a video prayerfully calling the parishioners and voting public to remember that who they vote for can be an act of caring for creation—or not.[8] Other organizations, such as KARIOS and Catholic Relief Services, also strive to educate and guide people to more just ways of living and loving, as Micah 6:8 proclaims: "To do justice, and to love kindness, and to walk humbly with your God." John Bullas, a KARIOS Sustainability Circle member and ordained minister with the United Church of Canada, recently offered a reflection on water that connected Exodus 7:1–7 and John 1:4–5, 13–14 with the practice of fracking that pollutes groundwater.[9] Catholic Relief services also offers resources and stories of hope to address water poverty.[10]

Laudato Si' educates believers that water is both a physical and spiritual good and thus, for Earth's sake and for the vulnerable in our world, we must pay attention to national and local practices and policies concerning water (*LS* 176). Do Christians notice that good water infrastructure is only accessible to the wealthy and consequences of poor environmental choices (e.g., Flint) are imposed upon less affluent communities that have little political and economic clout? Recent decisions by the U.S. government have put public lands under private control and put the protections built into the Water Act on hold. Shortsighted economic decisions are outweighing ecological, spiritual, social, and other common goods.[11] There are political implications to the message of justice and peace contained in the gospel. Consequently, Christians must engage in hard conversations and show some "tough" love. Caring for our common home must have a central place in our personal, social, political, and faith lives. *Laudato Si'* awakens and kindles a profound love of our Blue Marble, especially by an attitude of the heart that "accepts each moment as a gift from God to be lived to the full" (*LS* 226).

DAILY WATER EXAMEN

Over four hundred years ago, St. Ignatius of Loyola inspired people to a prayer-filled mindfulness via the Daily Examen. To conclude this section on water, let us prayerfully meditate on God's presence and an appreciation of water using the Examen.

A) **Become aware of God's presence.** Reflect on your encounter with the mystery of water in this chapter in the company of the Holy Spirit. The data, problems, Scripture, and passages from *Laudato Si'* may seem confusing to you—a blur, a jumble, a muddle. Ask God to bring clarity and understanding. Sit longer with areas where you felt God's voice speaking to you.

B) **Review the experience with gratitude.** Gratitude is the foundation of our relationship with God. Walk through your time exploring water in the presence of God and note its joys and delights. Focus on the gifts presented. Look at the wonderful and awful power of water. See the work you did, the knowledge you learned, the people you interacted with. What did you receive from these encounters? What did you give in return? Pay attention to small things—God is in the details.

C) **Pay attention to your emotions.** One of St. Ignatius's great insights was that we detect the presence of the Spirit of God in the movements of our emotions. Reflect on the feelings you experienced during your encounter with water. Wonder? Awe? Elation? Resentment? Compassion? Anger? Mystery? Confidence? What is God saying through these feelings?

D) **God will most likely show you some ways that you fell short.** Make note of your areas of water illiteracy. What brokenness has resulted from your illiteracy? But look deeply for other implications. Does a feeling of frustration perhaps mean that God wants you to consider a new direction in some area of your life? Are you concerned about a friend? The children of tomorrow?

E) **Choose one feature of the day and pray from it.** Ask the Holy Spirit to direct you to something during your encounter with water and *Laudato Si'* that God thinks is particularly important. It may involve a feeling—positive or negative. It may be a significant encounter with another person, creature, or element, or a vivid moment of pleasure or peace. Or it may be something that seems rather insignificant. Look at it. Pray about it. Allow the prayer to arise spontaneously from your heart—whether intercession, praise, repentance, or gratitude.

F) **Look toward tomorrow.** Ask God to give you flexibility and tenacity for tomorrow's challenges facing creation and humanity. What activity concerning water could you do differently? Pay attention to the feelings that surface as you survey what's coming up. Are you doubtful? Cheerful? Apprehensive? Full of delighted anticipation? Allow these feelings to turn into prayer. Seek your Creator for guidance as you love and live with water anew. Ask God for help and understanding. Pray for hope.

St. Ignatius encouraged people to talk to Jesus like a friend, so conclude the Daily Examen with a conversation with *Jesus, Living Water*. Explore the ways Jesus guides how you develop an authentic relationship with water. Ask forgiveness for your sins stemming from your water illiteracy and apathy. Ask for his protection and inspiration. Ask for his wisdom about the questions you have and the problems facing creation, including yourself as part of this watery world. Do all this in the spirit of gratitude. Your life is a gift and an expression of water's creativity and blessedness. End your Examen by praying the Our Father.

II

Earth

INTRODUCTION

> O dwellers in the dust, awake and sing for joy!
> For your dew is a radiant dew,
> and the earth will give birth to those long dead.
>
> Isaiah 26:19

As we learned in the first section, water brings life but not in isolation from the soil. Water chips away minerals and hijacks microbes from mountainsides, transporting them to the valleys where webs of life are woven together and human civilizations are built. We are dust dwellers and, hence, we need to appreciate the places where we live and move and have our being. We have forgotten that we are made of the dust of the stars and depend on all the dusty soil and souls around us. We must do some holy noticing and remember that Earth in all its magnificent forms was called "very good" by God. This is the truth of the incarnation: creation was so loved by its Creator that God chose to become a material being and participated uniquely in the cosmic love story. Why did we forget this? One reason is that we needed wood, coal, and minerals to fuel the industrial revolution, but exploiting Mother Earth seemed wrong. However, using (and abusing) a machine made of dead "matter" seemed almost justified—weren't machines made to benefit their human controllers? Thus, metaphors shifted to make us more comfortable with our exploitation. But some holy noticing will remind us of who and whose we are: whether it is when we play in nature, or when we see the same iron in both our blood and in rocks, or when we examine the interesting ways ants and mushrooms "talk" with one another, or when we hear a sermon on Adam's formation from *adamah* (dust). Each lesson reinforces that we are *terra animate*—animated Earth or soulful soil. This discovery should inform how we are to tend, serve, and protect the inspirited bodies of our neighbors, who also witness to a God who desires abundant life for all.

As Norman Wirzba and Fred Bahnson poignantly remind us in *Making Peace with the Land*, the Creator is intimately connected to creation and loves it. When we remain strangers to the land and hurt Earth's own ability to be creative, we are frustrating God's desire for abundant life for all. Matthew 25:40 affirms that when we feed and befriend those who are hungry, we are feeding and befriending Christ. But would we really feed

Jesus with the food collected from "spiritually tepid 'food drives' where we rifle through our pantries for cans of unpalatable food?"[1] Jesus deserves better than processed salt- and sugar-laden foods, and so do all those who hunger for food or companionship or love. We should aim for promoting abundant life and not merely starving off hunger or loneliness with quick, convenient fixes. This is not a criticism of frontline workers who are meeting the immediate hunger pangs of the bodies in front of them. But we must ask ourselves, Would we feed this food in this way to our own family every day? Does this way of feeding satisfy all our hungers and promote abundant life physically, socially, or spiritually? If we answer no, then we should dream bigger. This section is designed to help dusty souls notice the soils and souls around them and imagine new ways to promote abundant life. Chapter 4 will identify two earthy problems, which will be followed in the next chapter with an exploration of the powerful theological concept of the incarnation. By returning to our roots in *the fully divine and fully human* Jesus of Nazareth we can find the path to right relationship with our planet's many sacred bodies. The final chapter will explore several people and projects that are living the incarnational truth: we are earthy souls dwelling in the dust, inspired by the Spirit and loved abundantly by God.

Chapter 4

DISHING THE DIRT

What Is Happening to the Soil beneath Our Feet?

Earth is incredibly fertile, resilient, and beautiful and reveals something about God, Creator. The exuberance of Earth's urge to create is stunning. Four centuries ago people only imagined that there were only about ten thousand species of invertebrates, but today we know that in just the spider family there are more than thirty-eight thousand species. Even in a teaspoon of soil there are upward of 10 trillion bacteria representing as many as ten thousand species![1] Earth's urge to create is an expression of the abundant creativity of its Creator. But for the first time in planetary history, one species is hurting Earth's creativity and impairing her life systems: humans. There are many issues threatening Earth, but two are especially important: the loss of biodiversity and the shriveling of table fellowship.

LOSS OF BIODIVERSITY

> Each year sees the disappearance of thousands of plant and animal species which we will never know, which our children will never see, because they have been lost forever. The great majority become extinct for reasons related to human activity. Because of us, thousands of species will no longer give glory to God by their very existence, nor convey their message to us. We have no such right. (*LS* 32–33)

In chapter 1 of *Laudato Si'*, a special section is dedicated to the loss of biodiversity. This is not a surprise. In a 2016 report by the World Wildlife Foundation it was reported that vertebrate populations have declined by 58 percent between 1970 and 2012. The number of different animals living on land dropped by 38 percent and marine populations declined by 36 percent. The most alarming figure is that freshwater species have experienced on average an incredible 81 percent decline in that same period.[2] This means that only a small fraction of species of animals living in lakes, rivers, and wetlands in 1970 remain and every food chain has lost key pieces. The 2019 UN global assessment report only reaffirms the gravity of this problem: "Nature is declining globally at rates unprecedented in human history."[3]

In *Laudato Si'* Pope Francis tells us that shortsighted human economies and patterns of consumption have caused this loss of biodiversity (*LS* 32). God's divine revelation is dimmed when we destroy natural habitats to build the huge homes and buy all the stuff we think we need; or when we remain oblivious to where our electronics go when we throw them out; or when we use large amounts of water, pesticides, fossil fuels, and space to cultivate perfectly manicured lawns that do not feed people nor provide habitats for our animal neighbors. Our activities in the natural world often serve a very narrow form of business—one where natural resources and people are expendable and exploited to make bigger profits in the short term. It is our planetary neighbors and marginal human groups who are paying the high cost for this lifestyle (*LS* 34–41). We have no right to offload these costs onto others.

Pope Francis also speaks of the loss of biodiversity as a grave spiritual crisis. By preventing Earth's inhabitants from giving glory to God by their very existence, we become deaf to the majesty and love of our Creator (*LS* 33). Our ability to understand God, Jesus Christ, and the Holy Spirit diminishes when we degrade Earth and push animals and plants to extinction. We will act differently only when we show our love of God by loving our planetary neighbors. And in the end, we will also be loving ourselves better since our well-being is dependent on the well-being of our terrestrial neighbors. Loss of biodiversity detracts from our abundant life, prohibits our neighbors from having life, and fractures our relationship with God.

Review *Laudato Si'* 32–42 and then watch the following video made by Vandana Shiva, a physicist from India and protector of biological and cultural diversity: "Vandana Shiva Explains Clearly Why GMOs Are a Death Knell to Biodiversity and Farming" (https://www.youtube.com/watch?v=o_r6tHdZdhI). What was your initial reaction? How does she connect the loss of biodiversity with human suffering? How could your parish, school, or family care more for your terrestrial neighbors? Perhaps these ideas could be published in your church bulletin, or added to the petitions or sermon, or done during a family outing.

A frequently asked question at this point is whether our current loss of biodiversity, often called Earth's sixth mass extinction event, is just an inevitable part of life. The short answer is no. It is true that Earth has experienced the loss of massive numbers of species on five different occasions, but this was over a 4.5 billion-year history. These events were rare and happened at a slow enough rate that Earth could recover. What makes our current extinction event different is that it is happening so quickly—over a hundred or so years rather than millions. Another difference is humans are causing this extreme loss of biodiversity and no previous extinction event was caused by a single species. But if you ask most people, they cannot name one specific thing that they are doing to cause this extinction event. But small things, replicated millions of times by the seven billion human occupants of this planet, adds up. What we value and the activities we take part in, from the most mundane to the extraordinary, can help cultivate biodiversity or diminish it.[4]

To address our present extinction event, we need to humbly examine all aspects of our lives on Earth: agriculture, food, energy, logging, transportation, water, residential and commercial development, and pollution. We should celebrate what is good and change what is not. This will be hard, but our planetary family needs us and we, them.

ATROPHIED TABLE FELLOWSHIP

> We have to realize that a true ecological approach always becomes a social approach; it must integrate questions of justice in debates on the environment, so as to hear both the cry of the earth and the cry of the poor. (*LS* 49)

Laudato Si' astutely connects the demise of ecosystems with the decline in the quality of human life and breakdown of society. Our ecological crisis has social and spiritual dimensions that intersect; we cannot fix our biodiversity problem without concurrently healing human relationships (*LS* 119). Some U.S. statistics show the frayed edges of our society: in 2016, an estimated 2.2 million adolescents have had at least one major depressive episode.[5] On any given night in 2017, almost 9,000 people in North Carolina had no place to call home and in California the number is over 134,000.[6] In 2017, there were 8,524 cases of human trafficking, a modern day form of slavery, and this is almost a thousand more cases than the previous year.[7] In 2019, the American criminal justice system had more than 2.3 million people locked up in various institutions.[8] Sadly, in 2016 there were more than 42,000 overdose deaths caused by opioids, more than any previous year on record.[9] Another sobering fact is that 43.1 million Americans lived in poverty in 2016 and almost 6.1 million households did not have enough to eat most days. The Gospel of Matthew (25:1–40) teaches us that societies in need of healing have depressed, hungry, thirsty, homeless, lonely, poor, incarcerated, naked, vulnerable people. These sobering statistics show that our human family is crying out for healing and Earth echoes this cry.

How do the cries of Earth and the poor intertwine? Stories explain this best. When Earth's forest communities cry out as trees are being clear cut, local wells dry up, soil blows away, and people lose the ability to satisfy their hunger and thirst. When we pave over our landscapes and stop touching the natural world (*LS* 44), people lose the ability to satisfy our need to belong to something larger than ourselves. When we live in front of screens, people lose the ability to satisfy their longing for embodied relationships.[10] When Earth is imagined as only an object to be exploited, and anyone associated with Earth is expendable (*LS* 43), people lose their ability to satisfy their desire for community, meaningful work, and purpose. When beautiful spaces are only found in "safer" areas of cities (*LS* 45) while toxic areas are inflicted on poor neighborhoods, parents lose the ability to provide a good future for their children (*LS* 48). When the land loses its vitality after being besieged by pesticides, herbicides, and pollution, people lose the ability to satisfy their hunger and be healthy, creative citizens.

Watch the Greenbelt Movement's hope-filled response to atrophied table fellowship: (https://www.youtube.com/watch?v=BQU7JOxkGvo). Find out more about the founder of this movement, Nobel Peace Prize Winner Wangaari Maathai (http://www.greenbeltmovement.org/wangari-maathai). How could you improve the landscapes where you dwell and promote peace and justice?

People and places thrive together or diminish together, and this is best illustrated in our experience of food and table fellowship. We all eat—this fact connects all created life. Humans weave strong relationships as we break bread on the many tables of our lives: dinner tables, picnic tables, meeting tables, cafeteria tables, altar tables. We cannot have thriving, healthy human communities, economies, schools, and churches if the people in our neighborhoods, classrooms, and pews do not have access to good food that will nourish bodies, minds, and spirits. Food insecurity—or more simply put, hunger—is a result of shriveled table fellowship.

Holy noticing unearths who is the most vulnerable to becoming hungry. In U.S. households with children, single-parent homes (especially single women), women or men living alone, black, Hispanic, and low-income households are most at risk.[11] But surely the most fertile regions in the United States boast the most well-fed people? Unfortunately, no. North Carolina is home to some of the most fertile land in the United States, as well as to some of the most economically and socially distressed communities that experience food insecurity at alarming levels.[12] In a 2015 national ranking, North Carolina was the thirteenth worst food hardship state in the United States, with 17 percent of residents indicating that they struggled with hunger.

In addition, almost one-quarter of all North Carolina children under eighteen years of age experienced hunger on a regular basis. These are the "least" among us, and tackling the web of reasons for food insecurity is how to love as Matthew 25:40–45 commands. Pope Francis concurs: "We need to strengthen the conviction that we are one single human family. There are no frontiers or barriers, political or social, behind which we can hide, still less is there room for the globalization of indifference" (*LS* 52).

Explore the mission, vision, and philosophy of the community called Root Cause Farm in North Carolina: https://rootcausefarm.org/ (under "About"). What do you think of this table fellowship? Then read an article on L'Arche by Blake Mayes (May 13, 2019) in *America* magazine ("What Our Lonely Culture Can Learn from L'Arche, the Last Supper and 'Love Feasts,'" at https://www.americamagazine.org/faith/2019/05/13/what-our-lonely-culture-can-learn-larche-last-supper-and-love-feasts). How can the wisdom offered by the Lord's Acre and L'Arche become a part of your parish, school, or family life?

The root of the many societal problems is that we have forgotten who we are and how to grow and prepare our daily bread (*LS* 2). We must notice that we are both gardeners (those who care for the soil) and garden (we are dust and unto dust we shall return). We are both creators and part of creation. We are givers and gift. We are so disconnected from Earth that we are unable to notice the holiness of creation in its fragrance, flavor, and splendor. We are not in awe of what is being provided and by whom. Our table is bare, our hospitality hollow, and our fellowship impoverished. Diana Butler Bass, in her book *Grounded*,[13] reminds us about the sacred significance of ordinary table, the place where we form spiritual habits of hospitality, thankfulness, and gratitude. If we don't wake up, unsustainable ecological practices will continue and abundant life will allude human communities (*LS* 48–52).

But do Christians see food insecurity as a spiritual problem? North Carolina struggles with hunger, but more than three-quarters of North Carolinians belong to Christian denominations that have bread, food, or feeding the hungry as key components of how to live faithfully. They hear descriptions of Jesus as the bread of life (John 6:35) and pray to God to provide our daily bread. They partake in religious rituals and practices that occur around a table (e.g., Lord's Supper, grace before meals) and are reminded by prophets that planting gardens can address violence, poverty, and malnutrition (Jer 29).[14] Pope Francis indicates that the responses to the cries of the poor and Earth have been weak (*LS* 52–59), but this does not mean faith traditions cannot inspire a deep love of creation and the vulnerable humans (*LS* 64). *Laudato Si'* offers believers a way to value diversity and cultivate abundant table fellowship rooted in Jesus, the incarnation. This theology empowers us to reimagine ourselves as incarnational soil people living within a planetary family of inspirited dust.

Chapter 5

WISDOM FROM *LAUDATO SI'* TO GUIDE US

> Christ "chose to reach our intimate depths through a fragment of matter. He comes not from above, but from within, he comes that we might find him in this world of ours."
>
> *Laudato Si'* 236

This chapter investigates the powerful concept of the incarnation to promote a holy noticing of Earth's many bodies. The incarnation will guide us in our journey to remember and celebrate ourselves as both a gardener and garden. The truth of the incarnation is love—God's love for the dusty Earth, of which we are a part.

INCARNATION AS LOVE

The word *remember* is remarkable in that to "re"-member means to bring an idea from the past into the present. But if you see it beside its literary cousin, *dismember*, then *remember* can be understood as something that can be tangible and material rather than just an abstract idea. So, when Jesus said, "Do this in memory of me," it was not just an idea to think about on Sundays. We must make Jesus materially present by creating authentic table fellowship modeled after Christ's own life and ministry. This holy hospitality was made especially real at the Last Supper. This ordinary act of eating with his friends fed them, body and soul. At that table, Jesus gives the disciples a taste of how abundant life will be with God at the end-time. Our new scientific understanding of Earth does nothing to diminish the magnitude of this gift of grace. We now know that Earth's ecosystems sustain life because of sacrifice—one organism dies or ceases to be to feed another. This scientific truth resonates in John (12:24): "Very truly, I tell you, unless a grain of wheat falls into the earth and dies, it remains just a single grain; but if it dies, it bears much fruit." Jesus freely chose to embrace this darker aspect of life on Earth and model for us how sacrifice is part of both our vocations: gardener and garden. Thus, our holy noticing of this giving and receiving in Earth's ecosystems can heighten our awareness that the extinction of many species and diminishment of table fellowship is not Christlike reciprocity—we are not giving, only taking.

> As a group, read 2 Corinthians 8:7, 9, 13–15 and then consider the message of the parable of the Long Spoons (http://wefeedeachother.tumblr.com/activity). How do these stories speak to some of the challenges facing our common home outlined in the previous chapter? Where are the many tables where you experience fellowship in your life? Who do you invite to these tables? Why? Take time to explore the Christian Food Movement, which lives at the intersection of faith and farming: http://christianfoodmovement.org/about/. What could enrich your table fellowship and hospitality?

Remembering who and whose we are will help us to address our distorted belief that humanity alone has worth in God's eyes and thus, we need not be concerned about the welfare of Earth's many bodies. To remember who we are requires that we explore the dusty depths of the incarnation. Do we really appreciate the full humanity of the risen Jesus? If we do, we will realize that like us and other creatures, he was literally stardust and an extension of the land: the carbon in his body, oxygen in his lungs, calcium in his bones, and iron in his blood. His inspirited body interplayed with the Galilean landscape where he fed himself, sweat in the heat, hugged his mother, and played with his friends.

Holy noticing sees Jesus's membership in the whole family of creation, more specifically the human family, as a positive thing. The divinity of Jesus is not diminished by this. Rather, our appreciation for our ancient, dynamic world allows us to understand his divinity more; the man born in a stable is also the second person of the Trinity, who was present at the beginning of time and is working to draw all of creation toward its goal—wholeness or at-*one*-ment in God. Pope Francis speaks of this throughout *Laudato Si'*: "Christ has taken unto himself this material world and now, risen, is intimately present to each being, surrounding it with his affection and penetrating it with his light" (*LS* 221). "The ultimate destiny of the universe is in the fullness of God, which has already been attained by the risen Christ, the measure of the maturity of all things" (*LS* 83).

Some ask, why did he wait? Perhaps Jesus waited all those billions of years to become incarnate as a human for two reasons. First, he waited until the emergence of creatures with the capacity to choose to turn away from God. The flowers of the field or sparrow that falls to the ground cannot choose to turn from God, and as St. Francis noticed, in their life and death they were continually praising their Creator. Perhaps he also waited because we needed him to be embodied as a human to hear, see, and walk more fully with God. It is hard to be in an intimate relationship with another human, never mind a strange-looking arthropod or a tiny bacterium. So perhaps the divine manifestation in the blaze of the sun is too foreign to us (*LS* 85). God knew that we craved an intimacy that could only be satisfied with a relationship with a body that resembled our own. And God knew that with our ability to turn away, we would need even more guidance. However, our forgetfulness that we are both gardener and garden, mountain climber and mountain, has led us to believe that God is only in a relationship with us and the rest of creation does not matter. Perhaps we need to reflect on "Thinking Like a Mountain" by Aldo Leopold alongside *Laudato Si'* to remind us of the intimate relationship the Creator has with all of creation.

In 1949, Aldo Leopold wrote the article "Thinking Like a Mountain" as a counterpoint to common habits of seeing only short-term problems.... The narrative of every big mountain is long—whether millions of years of shifting tectonic plates, moving in slow inches, or repeated fiery blasts of molten rock. And every growing mountain reshapes old ecosystems.... Let us also invoke the memory of our Israelite forebears, who arranged their scriptures to begin with the heavens and the earth, the plants and the animals. All of biblical history occurs on hillsides, in valleys, alongside rivers and lakes. There are shepherds and fishers and people who turn trees into homes and furniture. When Isaiah envisions the world restored after all the human disruption has been corrected, he sees wolves and lambs, leopards and goats, lions and calves all living together. Many read that as a divinely imposed vegan revolution, but perhaps there is room there for acknowledging the significance of diversity....May we also invoke the memory of Jesus, the farmer (Mark 4:26–29). The apostles had probably gotten discouraged because they told people about Jesus a week or two before, yet the people were not remembering very well.... People are like plants in needing time to develop fully, and some need a lot more than others. Take the long view. Do not be discouraged...and meditate on three invocations of our forebears:

As long as there is growth, nurture it;
As long as you depend on good food and clean water, don't forget that it does not come from a store;
Learn how to think like a mountain.

(Dr. Edwin Bagley, professor of ethics and philosophy, Wingate University. Excerpt from an invocation given in 2016)

In chapter 2 of *Laudato Si'*, Pope Francis begins by reminding us that God said creation was very good right from the beginning and the cosmos never lost this designation, despite humanity's bad behavior. This point is crucial prior to any examination of the incarnation; as with any good book, when a reader jumps ahead vital nuances and plot lines are missed, skewing the reader's comprehension of the entire book. Deuteronomy (22:4, 6), Jeremiah (1:5), Leviticus (19 or 25), and the Psalms (24, 148, 104, and 136) support Pope Francis's claim that "the Bible has no place for tyrannical anthropocentrism unconcerned for other creatures" (*LS* 68). Sin is when we choose to inflict violence and abuse on others by abandoning the vulnerable and degrading nature (*LS* 66). The mystery of our unfolding universe can reattune us to the immense, cosmic horizon of God's love: "Soil, water, mountains; everything is, as it were, a caress of God" (*LS* 84). "From panoramic vistas to the tiniest living form, nature is a constant source of wonder and awe. It is also a continuing revelation of the divine" (*LS* 85). If we allow ourselves to reconnect with Earth's landscapes, we will discover God and *remember* who and whose we are—we are beloved, but so is the cosmos. The scales will fall from our eyes, and we will realize that our loss of biodiversity and shriveled table fellowship is indeed a spiritual crisis.

Read aloud or listen to the story "Old Turtle and the Broken Truth" by Douglas Wood (https://www.youtube.com/watch?v=3GTYbsI6UYE). Then listen to the hymn "For the Beauty of the Earth" and worship music "When You Walk into the Room" by Bryan and Katie Torwalt (https://www.youtube.com/watch?v=8Zqg5k_GUx4). Let the words wash over your senses. What parts of these stories of love resonate with the truth of the incarnation presented in paragraphs 84 and 85 of *Laudato Si'*? Do you see your relation to all other creatures differently? Do you see your relationship with Christ differently? What does this move you to do differently?

The imaginative work of holy noticing our common home culminates in the section of *Laudato Si'* that speaks about the incarnation ("The Gaze of Jesus," *LS* 96–100). This section tells the stories of Jesus's life and ministry in light of our cosmic communion. Jesus's full humanity speaks of God's love (Matt 6:26; 11:25; Luke 12:6). His stopping to appreciate the fertility of Earth's fields and using even the smallest seed to explain the good news speaks to the goodness of creation announced in Genesis (John 4:35; Matt 13:31–32). Jesus's talent for reforming wood into tools for human life (Mark 6:3) also speaks to the instrumental worth of natural resources. Pope Francis reminds us that "Christ is at work in a hidden manner in the natural world as a whole" (*LS* 99). This is hard to grasp unless you look at his earthy ministry. Jesus healed broken bodies, families, communities, and spirits. With his mixing of saliva and soil together, Jesus healed diseased, marginalized bodies; with the touching of his robe, or a command—or the sharing of bread, wine, and fish—sickness, division, and loneliness were healed; and with the performing of miracles on mountaintops, beside lakes, in the wilderness, and on a hillside populated by olive trees, Jesus healed sagging spirits. Thus, Jesus's birth, life, ministry, passion, death, and resurrection can speak of the goodness of creation and his deep love of our beautiful and broken world. Often people of faith see Jesus's incarnation as a necessary evil. They think Jesus merely tolerated being born and was impatient to be done with his material body. *Laudato Si'* is clear that this is not the case: "The flowers of the field and the birds which his human eyes contemplated and admired are now imbued with his radiant presence" (*LS* 100). Thus, the earthly and risen Christ is immensely fond of inspirited bodies.

Chapter 6

LIVING *LAUDATO SI'*

How to Care for Our Terrestrial Neighbors

Embracing the incarnation requires a high level of holy noticing and love of neighbor. Do we see the mustard seeds, wheat in a field, dragonflies, water, or soil as places where God is present? Do we understand all of creation as a beautiful, diverse, universal family worthy of "sacred, affectionate and humble respect?" (*LS* 89). This potent holy noticing requires a change of heart inspired by the truth of the earthly and risen Christ. Improving holy noticing skills is the way seminaries and places of formation can provide what Pope Francis desires: "An education in responsible simplicity of life, in grateful contemplation of God's world, and in concern for the needs of the poor and the protection of the environment" (*LS* 214). Fortunately, there are many examples of people and projects loving soil and souls to be our guides on this new path.

Many recognize that biodiversity loss and the increase in poverty and hunger are parts of the same vicious cycle. Some faith traditions are beginning to appreciate the connection between conservation of species and loving your human neighbors, and are making creation care a priority. Why is this faith-conservation connection important? Over four billion people (nearly two-thirds of the world's population) are affiliated with mainstream faith traditions and live in countries where there is a rapid loss of biodiversity. If more people appreciated creation as sacred space rather than dead space, perhaps things could really change.[1] Christians need to use their love of Jesus to ignite a deep love of the birds, bees, and other bodies that co-dwell in the landscapes where churches are built. This is incarnational hospitality. St. Gabriel's Parish in Toronto has embraced a greening of sacred space through the design of architect Roberto Chiotti and ecotheological principles of Passionist priest Fr. Thomas Berry. The medium is the message, as philosopher Marshall McLuhan rightly noted, and since creation gives glory to God, then our worship spaces ought to allow the natural spaces where we co-dwell to inform and inspire building and liturgical practices.

ACTIVITY: Watch the 15-minute video about St. Gabriel's Parish and Roberto Chiotti: https://www.youtube.com/watch?v=G-Z0HvgorPc. Think about what theological message the physical worship space is conveying. How could creation teach theology at your parish? How could you green the sacred spaces in and around your church?

Individual parishes have also stepped up and found creative ways to live the incarnational truth of *Laudato Si'*. For example, St. Eugene's parish in Asheville, North Carolina has a Creation Care Ministry, and they have creatively responded to the call to respect our planet and its many inhabitants. They have created educational opportunities by hosting booths on honey gathering, habitat care, energy conservation, and recycling goals for the parish. They have changed their consumptive practices by reducing the use of disposable bags in the church and in the homes of parishioners, and have eliminated the use of Styrofoam cups at parish social gatherings. They also cultivate holy noticing in their parishioners, young and old, by having events where people can create a bird's nest bag, grow and care for seedlings, and experience the benefits of an electric car. They have changed infrastructure at the church to included solar panels and created fruitful dialogues within and outside of the church (e.g., National Audubon Society, Energy Innovative Task Force, Energy Savers Network, and other churches) to spread the good news.[2]

Another key step to living the incarnational truth of *Laudato Si'* is to amplify our holy noticing of "our daily bread" and use our insights to inform how we partake in this daily activity. Do you know where your food came from? What creatures or growers gifted you with your last meal? And who are you breaking bread with? The daily habit of prayerful hospitality around the many tables of our lives—boardroom table, school desk, picnic table, dinner table—can bring us closer to our truest selves as both gardeners and gardens. Perhaps hospitality is asking a coworker to join you for tea, providing hungry college students with a treat at the start of an exam, creating a safe space for people made vulnerable by a lack of compassion, or starting a community garden that is accessible for those with disabilities. Faithfulness to the truth of the incarnation means that we use our many talents and roles in our communities to demand that creation care be taken seriously.

Christians can balance caring for Earth and caring for the word, two ways to faithfully feed people. Both are necessary for abundant life. This dual approach to caring for inspirited bodies and building communion occurs at the Anatoth Garden (North Carolina). It is named after the garden plot in Jeremiah (29:5–7) that signifies both a place of friendship and the process of establishing peace.[3] Incarnational truth also grounds the Food and Faith program offered by N.C. Resourceful Communities. This program was initiated to provide rural churches with the training, support, resources, and grant money to support innovative grass roots initiatives and build fruitful partnerships to address food insecurity. The uniqueness of this program is its triple bottom-line approach: serving one's community means balancing and promoting ecological, social, and economic well-being.[4] Another program cultivating real table fellowship is Food That LAUGHS. Developed by the ministry Life Around the Table,[5] the program curriculum is rooted in the story of Sarah, who laughs skeptically when she hears of God's plan to give her a son, and later, she laughs in delight and joy when God gives her the experience of being a mother; "Sarah is a model to us of God's provision and promise in our own lives, regardless of seemingly barren circumstances. God is a good. God has created a good world which has fallen but having been redeemed through Jesus Christ we celebrate life with joy, promise, and hope. Central to celebrating life is eating together."[6] LAUGHS is an acronym for *local, affordable, uncomplicated, good, healthy,* and *seasonal*—all important parts of holy noticing the food that sustains our bodies. When we embrace the guiding principles of Food That LAUGHS and come around the tables of our lives to listen to Earth's many bodies, we strengthen planetary fellowship across human, landscape, and species boundaries. Delighting in good food and friends is the essence of incarnational life.

Research L'Arche (https://www.larche.org/what-we-do; https://www.larcheusa.org/) and then watch "The Heart of L'Arche" (Washington, DC). Take notice of the many forms of celebration and table fellowship (https://www.youtube.com/watch?v=YjnRtH_MHB8). How can L'Arche communities teach your parish or family how to care for creation better?

Another creative way of generating authentic table fellowship at an international level is being done by ECHO: Educational Concerns for Hunger Organization. This organization has a specific, Christ-centered mission. To follow Jesus means reducing hunger and improving lives worldwide through partnerships that equip people with agricultural resources and skills. Its vision of honoring God by empowering others through sustainable agriculture is an example of a deep love of soulful soil. ECHO is a place where anyone can go to get good information about how to feed bodies and communities. Its research into how shantytowns can support rooftop gardening using materials easily scrounged in poorer neighborhoods is just one example of its innovation inspired by the creative Spirit.[7]

A loss of biodiversity and the erosion of human communities go hand in hand and is a symptom of a deep hunger for authentic love. To address this longing, we must become better holy noticers and more attentive students of the incarnation. The incarnational truth of *Laudato Si'* reminds us that Christ's love for the wild and messily created world extends from the stable in Bethlehem back to the Big Bang, and from the cross forward to the end of time. If we remember this, we will share in God's delight of Earth's many dusty bodies and live faithfully as images of a hospitable, loving God.

DAILY EARTH EXAMEN

Over four hundred years ago, St. Ignatius of Loyola inspired people to a prayer-filled mindfulness via the Daily Examen. To conclude this section on Earth, let us prayerfully meditate on God's presence and an appreciation of Earth using the Examen.

A) **Become aware of God's presence.** Reflect on your encounter with the mystery of Earth and your selfhood—soil and soul—in this chapter in the company of the Holy Spirit. The data, problems, Scripture, and passages from *Laudato Si'* may seem confusing to you—a blur, a jumble, a muddle. Ask God to bring clarity and understanding. Sit longer with areas where you felt God's voice speaking to you.

B) **Review the experience with gratitude.** Gratitude is the foundation of our relationship with God. Walk through your time exploring Earth in the presence of God and note your joys and delights. Focus on the gifts presented. Look at the wonder and power of Earth and inspirited bodies. See the work you did, the knowledge you learned, the bodies you interacted with. What did you receive from these encounters? What did you give in return? Pay attention to small things—God is in the details.

C) **Pay attention to your emotions.** One of St. Ignatius's great insights was that we detect the presence of the Spirit of God in the movements of our emotions. Reflect on the feelings you experienced during your encounter with Earth. Wonder? Awe? Elation? Resentment? Compassion? Anger? Mystery? Confidence? What is God saying through these feelings?

D) **God will most likely show you some ways that you fell short.** Make note of your areas of illiteracy concerning Earth. What brokenness has resulted from your lack of knowledge or appreciation of Earth. But look deeply for other implications. Does a feeling of frustration perhaps mean that God wants you to consider a new direction in some area of your life? Are you concerned about a friend? About the children of tomorrow?

E) **Choose one feature of the day and pray from it.** Ask the Holy Spirit to direct you to something during your encounter with Earth's inspirited bodies and *Laudato Si'* that God thinks is particularly important. It may involve a feeling—positive or negative. It may be a significant encounter with another person, creature, or element, or a vivid moment of pleasure or peace. Or it may be something that seems rather insignificant. Look at it. Pray about it. Allow the prayer to arise spontaneously from your heart—whether intercession, praise, repentance, or gratitude.

F) **Look toward tomorrow.** Ask God to give you strength and wisdom for tomorrow's challenges facing creation and humanity. What activities connected to Earth could you do differently? Pay attention to the feelings that surface as you survey what's coming up. Are you doubtful? Cheerful?

Apprehensive? Full of delighted anticipation? Allow these feelings to turn into prayer. Seek your Creator for guidance as you love soil and souls, gardeners and gardens, and live a dusty, incarnational existence anew. Ask God for help and understanding. Pray for hope.

St. Ignatius encouraged people to talk to Jesus like a friend, so conclude the Daily Examen with a conversation with *Jesus, incarnate*. Explore the ways Jesus guides how you develop an authentic relationship with Earth. Ask forgiveness for your sins stemming from your illiteracy and apathy. Ask for his protection and inspiration. Ask for his wisdom about the questions you have and the problems facing creation, including yourself as part of this dusty world. Do all this in the spirit of gratitude. Your life is a gift and an expression of Earth's creativity and blessedness. End your Examen by praying the Hail Mary, a prayer to the Mother of the incarnate Jesus.

III

Air

INTRODUCTION

> I could compare my music to white light which contains all colors. Only a prism can divide the colors and make them appear; this prism could be the spirit of the listener.
>
> Arvo Pärt

On our planet, air is our constant companion. It animates our bodies and allows us to speak when its moves across our vocal cords. But how do you describe what cannot be seen but can be heard as it rustles the leaves in the trees and can be felt so powerfully as a tornado effortlessly contorts metal? Science can describe oxygen gas as the elegant dance of two oxygen atoms and explain bird flight as a cocreative adventure of wing and air. But human imaginations need both science and art to fully appreciate the wonder of Earth's atmosphere. One composer, Arvo Pärt, captured the essence of air in his composition called "Spiegel im Spiegel"—Mirror in the Mirror.

> Take time to listen to "Spiegel im Spiegel" and absorb the simplicity of the notes, the cadence of the music, and ascent and descent of notes: https://www.youtube.com/watch?v=aS7qmtQLSyY. What do you sense? How could this music help you imagine the Holy Spirit?

This piece of almost weightless music transcends cultures or backgrounds, moving people from all walks of life. Those who are open to its expansiveness are invited to a place of serenity. But the music also demands a response. For some, this piece creates in them the desire to breathe deeply as the music cascades over their senses. It is gentle and meditative; it cannot help but slow the frenzy of your own life, even just for a few minutes. The deliberate pace of this music invites the audience to do the creative, introspective, intuitive work of holy noticing that we are often too busy to do. For others, this music is like a slow heartbeat as it pulses through life's ups and downs. Our breathing and circulatory systems share a cooperative cadence, and life is sustained only when they work together. Thus, our bodies seem intimately attuned to this composition; it matches the vital time signature of our hearts. Commentators indicate that there is virtually nothing to this airy piece, only "the slow steady arpeggios on the piano" that work together with the "ascending and descending scales on the cello." But in its etherealness, they are brought to tears without knowing why. Perhaps their emotion stems from primordial memories of when spirit and matter intertwined during the first few moments of creation. Our common origin story told by Genesis and modern science reminds us of the primal lullaby of Spirit and matter—an aspect of life lost on imaginations formed by the rigid rationality bequeathed by Enlightenment thinkers. The Enlightenment emphasis of separation, fragmentation of knowledge, difference, and human supremacy have numbed us. But opening ourselves to this primordial lullaby will set our imaginations free. Its simplicity and provocativeness liberate us to fully contemplate the movement of the animating Spirit that once moved in the same manner over the water, bringing order, cadence—and life—to the world.

But what if air, shared through the centuries, is not life-giving? Would our imaginations still be able to make sense of how the animating Spirit is working in our midst to bring life from death? The problem of air pollution has theological dimensions worth pursuing. Liberation from what is choking us—literally and spiritually—comes when we recognize our common origin, interconnected present, and shared destiny. Past, present, and future is woven together by the Spirit. Chapter 7 will explore what is happening to our planet's atmosphere, followed by an overview of the theology of Holy Spirit in *Laudato Si'*. This leads into chapter 9, a hope-filled exploration of those laboring with the Spirit to create paths to abundant life by addressing air pollution.

Chapter 7

WAITING TO EXHALE

What Is Happening in the Skies above Us?

> Since everything is closely interrelated, and today's problems call for a vision capable of taking into account every aspect of the global crisis, I suggest that we now consider some elements of an integral ecology, one which clearly respects its human and social dimensions.
>
> *Laudato Si'* 137

Would it surprise you to know that approximately 3.5 billion years ago, there was no oxygen gas in the atmosphere and no life as we know it today? We are indebted to many ancient microorganisms (blue-green algae) for our existence because billions of years ago, they pumped oxygen into our oceans and atmosphere as they transformed sunshine into energy. Thanks to their efforts and others like them, the air in Earth's atmosphere is approximately 78 percent nitrogen gas and 21 percent oxygen, but it also has small amounts of other gases, too, such as carbon dioxide, neon, and hydrogen.[1] Although air is primarily gas, it can also contain small living organisms (e.g., bioaerosols), particles (e.g., dust, pollen, chemicals), and water molecules (e.g., the cause of mugginess on a humid day). Earth's atmosphere also protects us from too much heat or cold, from meteors, and from harmful rays from the sun. There are many intriguing things about air, but one stands out. Every single breath you take has been associated with another living organism. At the level of atoms, we can say with confidence that the oxygen atoms we breathe in once belonged to a leg of a dinosaur or was present in the lungs of Aristotle or even Jesus. The same is true for other atoms. "There may have been a carbon atom in last night's cupcake that was once integral to the structure of Julius Caesar's left toenail."[2] Our world only has a limited number of atoms to go around. So, if we significantly change what is in the air by adding pollutants and toxic materials, it is cause for grave concern.

AIR POLLUTION

Thankfully, the EPA indicates that there is less air pollution than when they first introduced the Clean Air Act in 1971. But there are still areas in the United States that exceed national air quality standards for at least one of the six most common pollutants: surface level ozone, particle pollution, carbon monoxide, lead, sulfur dioxide, and nitrogen dioxide.[3] More recent scientific data has shown that methane gas is almost eighty times worse than carbon dioxide for trapping heat. Methane is a byproduct of the oil and gas industry, is a primary component of sheep and cow belches and flatulence, and is created when food decays in landfills. A significant problem with air pollution is that it can travel much longer distances than water or ground pollution and wreaks havoc across state and country boundaries. Thus, industrial nations cannot afford to turn a blind eye to air pollution.

Read the following *National Geographic* article on methane and cows: Rebecca Rupp, "A Sprinkle of Seaweed Could Deflate Gassy Cows," Nov. 29, 2019, https://www.nationalgeographic.com/culture/food/the-plate/2016/11/seaweed-may-be-the-solution-for-burping-cows/. Then watch the following about innovative ways of dealing with methane gas emitted by food waste: "Colorado Is Using Piles of Rotting Food for Fuel," CNN Business, Oct. 6, 2016, https://www.youtube.com/watch?time_continue=74&v=6isTQQa0afk. What food choices could you make to help curb methane production and the clear cutting of forests to graze cattle? How could this be part of your prayer life and the spiritual activity of cultivating virtue?

Air pollution is measured with the air quality index (AQI). The lower the index number, the cleaner the air. The consensus is that an AQI of 50 is good,[4] but NASA scientists claim that if you are outdoors with the AQI over 100, it would be like breathing car exhaust all day—this air is definitely not life-giving. In the United States, the American Lung Association publishes an annual "State of the Air" report to keep readers informed. In 2018 it found that ozone pollution is getting worse, but particle pollution is getting better. However, it also offered a staggering statistic: "The number of people exposed to unhealthy levels of air pollution increased to more than 133.9 million people."[5] This is almost 9 million more than the year before.[6] If you are one of these millions of people, you may experience premature death, developmental harm, asthma attacks, lung cancer, wheezing, coughing, cardiovascular harm, increased susceptibility to infections, and lung tissue damage.[7] Air pollution can also impact how your brain functions, as reported by

National Geographic.[8] Less affluent and marginalized racial and ethnic groups consistently face greater harm from air pollution because they have fewer choices about where they can live, poorer job opportunities, less access to healthcare, schools, and grocery stores, and less political clout to ensure sources of pollution are not placed in their neighborhoods.[9]

> Watch the following video: Aliya Barnwell, "A Chinese Artist Made a Solid Brick of Pollution by Vacuuming Smog out of the Air," Digital Trends, Dec. 9, 2015, https://www.digitaltrends.com/photography/chinese-artist-brick-of-pollution/. What did you feel after watching how this artist creatively awoke people to the problem of air pollution? How does your faith speak to caring for our atmosphere?

Our avian neighbors are also harmed by air pollution. The lungs of birds, bats, and other respiring creatures are negatively impacted by particulates they breathe in. Continual exposure to vehicle exhaust can lead to reduced egg production and hatching rates, increased abandonment, and overall growth reduction in birds.[10] Photo pollution (artificial light) also poses a grave risk to our airborne friends due to the confusion they experience over day and night. Some birds move away from feeding spots because of artificial lighting and thus starve to death. Another grave threat to bird life is collisions with glass buildings. Glass windows are worse than invisible because they reflect foliage or the sky, and to birds, they look like a good place to fly. The sheer number of windows in low-rises, high-rises, and residences kill hundreds of millions to billions of birds annually in the United States thanks to these collisions.[11]

Some human activities that significantly increase air pollution include the intentional burning of forests to make room for crops, wildfires brought on by hotter, drier climates (or the careless tossing of a cigarette out of a window), emissions from coal-fired power plants, vehicle exhaust, and the production of methane. Since air pollution travels far distances, the political actions of one state or country can impact many communities. Take the removal of lead from gasoline as a positive example. Initially this legislation was resisted, but the Clean Air Act incentivized the gradual phasing out of leaded gas, with a total ban taking effect on January 1, 1996. Thus, thanks to the fortitude of many, "thousands of tons of lead have been removed from the air, and blood levels of lead in our children are down 70 percent. This means that millions of children will be spared the painful consequences of lead poisoning, such as permanent nerve damage, anemia or mental retardation."[12] A negative example involves political leaders beginning a process of rolling back the U.S. Clean Car Standards in May of 2018[13] and restricting other state-level regulations that limit the pollutants coming out of tailpipes into the air. The reason given is to release auto manufacturers from the financial burden of producing innovative ways to diminish fuel use. This, they claim, will boost our economy, which is a powerful argument. But how can we have viable, healthy economies with strong businesses in communities where the people are sick with lung and heart diseases? Can we not have innovation, jobs, and a healthy environment? The answer is yes! People of faith must ask themselves if this detrimental type of economic development contributes to God's vision of abundant life for all. If not, then we need to be inspired by the Spirit and look for innovative ways to meet the transportation needs of our communities. The theology of the Holy Spirit found in *Laudato Si'* can help.

Chapter 8

WISDOM FROM *LAUDATO SI'* TO GUIDE US

> The Spirit of God has filled the universe with possibilities and therefore, from the very heart of things, something new can always emerge.
>
> *Laudato Si'* 80

Laudato Si' affirms that our transcendent Creator God is intimately present to each being, without interfering with the freedom of any creature (*LS* 79–80). The earthly and risen Christ also companions the created world, both at the beginning of time, during his life on Earth, and at the end of time thanks to his universal Lordship (Col 1:19–20; 1 Cor 15:28). Earth's flora and fauna, even the birds Jesus contemplated and admired, "are now imbued with his radiant presence" (*LS* 100). However, it is the essence and creative work of the Holy Spirit that helps us make sense of God's continued presence and activity in the world to promote abundant life. As we notice the movement of the redeeming Spirit in our world, we can see her creative, liberating work: in the new blossoms on trees after the harshest winter; or the birth of a new island after the blistering eruption of a volcano on the seafloor; or in the lusty brawl of a newborn child ripe with potential; or in a new, often unsettling way of living contrary to the status quo; or even the healing discovered after sin. All in all, the Spirit is with us in our broken, beautiful world, moving us all toward communion with God as we pray each Sunday: "on earth as it is in heaven."

"It's a beautiful thing to see the presence of the Holy Spirit working amidst brokenness. Life has been a crazy, emotional ride for a while now and it has honestly been so hard to see God moving. So hard to believe that He was moving mountains on my behalf. So hard to remember to praise Him in the valleys when I was at rock bottom.

But where I am today is not where I was last month. Who I am right now in this moment is a world of difference from the broken girl I was when I came home from school in June.

I no longer have a desire to end my own life.

To say I wholeheartedly love every ounce of my life is an understatement—I'm so grateful for the life, family, and friends I have been given.

The craziest part about every bit of this is that the Holy Spirit was within me in the valley lows *and* the mountain highs. The grace and love never changed. While it was hard to see in the lows, from this view on top, I can see it all. I can see God carrying me through each. and. every. low. I can see the endless grace constantly pursuing me and His reckless love constantly chasing me.

When you think it can only get worse, just look. Remember that you have the Holy Spirit within you, a God that loves you going before you, and a perfect Savior covering you in endless grace, love, and mercy."
(Mary Katherine Williams, undergraduate student at Wingate University, social media post 2018)

Laudato Si' presents the Holy Spirit as a divine inner presence, an "interior impulse" (*LS* 216), an ultimately creative, empowering, and liberating force that enables us to discern God's message of salvation in the cosmos and act on it (*LS* 80, 211, 221). The first focus of this chapter is organized around two key passages that highlight the Holy Spirit in *Laudato Si'*:

> The Holy Spirit can be said to possess an *infinite creativity*, proper to the divine mind, which knows how to *loosen the knots of human affairs*, including the most complex and inscrutable. (80)

> The Spirit, *infinite bond of love*, is *intimately present* at the very heart of the universe, *inspiring and bringing new pathways*. (238; my italics)

INFINITE CREATIVITY AND BOND OF LOVE

Through the infinite creativity of the Holy Spirit, all of creation is inspired, nourished, and healed—if we do not inhibit this sacred, creative impetus. The Spirit, appreciated as infinite creativity, can help humanity awaken to our destructive ways so that together with Earth's own creative impetus, we can forge a better future and live up to our true potential as images of God. If we are made in the image of this Creative Spirit, then our oppression of Earth's creativity—and our own—is not who we are nor what we are called to do.

Human affairs are full of knots or challenges, and what is promised by the Spirit is not a life *without* knots (suffering and death). Rather, the breath of God offers abundant life *despite* the knots of sinful human affairs or those that are inevitable aspects of our finite world (e.g., old age, sickness) (*LS* 234). God loves so abundantly that he chooses to be present during times of darkness and light (Matt 10:29) and is always working to liberate the oppressed and heal the broken. Today we are failing the human species, our planet, and God because a "technological paradigm" has captivated our imaginations and (mis)guided our actions (*LS* 106–14). This way of looking at the world affirms that humans are masters of the created world. And thanks to technology, we are powerful enough to change the face of our planet (e.g., the removal of entire tops of mountains) and interrupt natural systems (e.g., climate change) (*LS* 216).

Watch the trailer for the 2006 documentary "Manufactured Landscapes": https://www.youtube.com/watch?time_continue=14&v=KVybNCPzG7M. What did you notice? How have we changed Earth's landscapes? How does *Laudato Si'* speak to this manufacturing of Earth's landscapes? If you have time, watch the entire documentary and reflect on human and ecosystem impacts of our industrialized world.

This paradigm is fueled by a radical individualism, human centeredness, and a sense of spiritual superiority. We think we don't have any knots or that we can fix them without help. This way of seeing ourselves is so pervasive and unchallenged, says Pope Francis, that it is diminishing our freedom and creativity as well as frustrating the creativity of Earth and the Holy Spirit (*LS* 108). "The external deserts in the world are growing, because the internal deserts have become so vast" (*LS* 217). Despite our blindness and roadblocks, the Holy Spirit never stops trying to loosen the knots we have created and move us to new activities that promote abundant life for all. Pope Francis admits that Christians have not always appreciated the spiritual treasures we have been bestowed, nor have we grasped how the "life of the spirit is not dissociated from the body or from nature or from worldly realities" (*LS* 216). The Spirit lives in and with us, in communion with all that surrounds us. She shows us that true creative power is not power over but *em*powerment, which is only possible when we live in communion with others. Thus, our ecological crisis may have two silver linings: our crisis is forcing us toward a deeper appreciation of the Spirit who unites Earth's many bodies, and inspiring us to embrace our vocation as cocreators who can dream up innovative ways of loving our cosmic family.

Our polluted skies and scarred lungs of our marginalized human kin signal a dryness of our interior spiritual life, one lacking love. A Christian spirituality anchored by an infinite bond of love—a divine love "intimately present at the very heart of the universe"—will breathe new life into how we care for our common home. Appreciation of the Holy Spirit as "infinite bond of love" comes from a great pastor and teacher from the past: St. Augustine. Like us, Christians in the early church required help to understand the mystery of the Trinity (always one *and* three). St. Patrick used a three-leaf shamrock, but St. Augustine used John's vision of God as Love as a way of describing the Trinity: Lover (Creator), Beloved (Jesus), Love (Spirit) (1 John 4:8). This model allowed the unity and difference of the Trinity to remain coupled together. You cannot be a lover without someone to love, nor can you be beloved if there is no one to love you, nor is any of this possible without love itself. *Laudato Si'* emphasizes that the love of the Trinity overflows into all of creation (*LS* 238), making the world very good indeed. The love that bonds the divine family is the source of what connects all of us as a planetary family: "When our hearts are authentically open to universal communion, this sense of fraternity excludes nothing and no one" (*LS* 92). The Holy Spirit unites us with all who have preceded us and those who will come after us in our human family and with our brother sun, sister moon, brother river, and mother earth. Humanity is not the only part of creation that God loves (*LS* 84). Together, the Spirit inspires us all to create abundant webs of life. Our membership in this "splendid universal communion" means that everyone and everything has a place and a purpose in this world (*LS* 220). The Holy Spirit as Love also demands that loving relationships be cocreative: a sincere Lover seeks the well-being of the beloved and vice versa. Love cannot be one sided, self-serving, or destructive. And when we love our neighbors, we are loving ourselves and vice versa. The Holy Spirit inspires Christians to be courageous, as our foremothers and forefathers were, and channel our creative energies away from oppressive ways of thinking and destructive actions toward paths of peace, justice, and preservation of our atmosphere (*LS* 92).

> Human beings, while capable of the worst, are also capable of rising above themselves, choosing again what is good, and making a new start, despite their mental and social conditioning. We are able to take an honest look at ourselves, to acknowledge our deep dissatisfaction, and to embark on new paths to authentic freedom. No system can completely suppress our openness

> to what is good, true and beautiful, or our God-given ability to respond to his grace at work deep in our hearts. (*LS* 205)

HUMAN IDENTITY AND PURPOSE

The second focus of this chapter concerns the affirmation in *Laudato Si'* that the Spirit is not only an inner, creative impulse that unites the cosmos, but she *defines who we are and what we do as human creatures*. Since we are made in the image and likeness of a relational, creative, loving God, "we are always capable of going out of ourselves toward the other. Unless we do this, other creatures will not be recognized for their true worth; we are unconcerned about caring for things for the sake of others; we fail to set limits on ourselves in order to avoid the suffering of others or the deterioration of our surroundings" (*LS* 208). Thus, human activities glorify God when they are an extension of the work of the creative Spirit: empowering, liberating, love centered (*LS* 93–95). A Christian ecological spirituality can fuel a "passionate concern for the protection of our world," but Pope Francis claims that this spirituality cannot be sustained by just *knowing* Christian doctrine (*LS* 216). This does not imply that we disregard our doctrinal treasures. Rather, an ecological Christian spirituality must be fed by many sources: by Scripture, Christian doctrines, scientific and artistic descriptions of the created universe, a prayerful immersion in Earth's landscapes, waterways, and skies, relationships, and activities that cultivate ecological virtue.

> Yet education, aimed at creating an "ecological citizenship," is at times limited to providing information, and fails to instill good habits....Only by cultivating sound virtues will people be able to make a selfless ecological commitment.... There is a nobility in the duty to care for creation through little daily actions and it is wonderful how education can bring about real changes in lifestyle. Education in environmental responsibility can encourage ways of acting which directly and significantly affect the world around us, such as avoiding the use of plastic and paper, reducing water consumption, separating refuse, cooking only what can reasonably be consumed, showing care for other living beings, using public transport or car-pooling, planting trees, turning off unnecessary lights, or any number of other practices. All of these reflect a generous and worthy creativity which brings out the best in human beings. Reusing something instead of immediately discarding it, when done for the right reasons, can be an act of love which expresses our own dignity. (*LS* 211)

Every small, daily act of care can cultivate Spirit-inspired ecological virtue, but they are not enough. These personal expressions also must be integrated into civic and political life; "social love moves us to devise larger strategies to halt environmental degradation and to encourage a 'culture of care' which permeates all of society" (*LS* 231).

Christian spirituality demands a loving lifestyle that recognizes, respects, and seeks the well-being of the "other" in big and small ways.

Watch *Covenant* (https://vimeo.com/2970560), a short film about people from diverse religious traditions coming together to fight for clean air. Explore how these religious leaders put their faith into action and helped organize a grassroots movement that eventually helped ensure that the air we breathe remained clean. How does this connect to the essence of the Holy Spirit referred to in *Laudato Si'*? Be sure to also look at the title, *Covenant*, and discuss how creation care can connect with what you understand the word *covenant* to mean.

The following chapter shows how people are living their vocation as images of God. Their deep love of and for others demonstrate how churches can be truly "on fire" with the Spirit and promote abundant life for all.

Chapter 9

LIVING *LAUDATO SI'*

How to Care for Our Neighbors in the Skies

> In any discussion about a proposed venture, a number of questions need to be asked in order to discern whether or not it will contribute to genuine integral development. What will it accomplish? Why? Where? When? How? For Whom? What are the risks? What are the costs? Who will pay those costs and how?
>
> *Laudato Si'* 185

The questions asked above by Pope Francis have deep spiritual roots. If we are animated by love, and this is what unites us, then all conversations concerning human identity, purpose, and development ought to ask these "love" questions. Pope Francis is clear that there is an urgent need for "frank dialogue" in politics and economics—how we organize human interaction and distribute the goods in society—to determine whether they are in the service of life or not. Do they promote the fullness of life for all or stifle "human creativity" (*LS* 190)? Living in harmony with creation is the fullest expression of human life and creativity because it gives witness to the Holy Spirit and to the shalom that awaits at end-time (Isa 11; Rev 21). Pope Francis and other faith leaders have also called attention to a prevalent myth, namely, that caring for creation means that you cannot make a good living, lead a happy life, or be a faithful parishioner and citizen. It is not either creation care or financial security—it must be both/and. We just need to imagine and create new ways to live in harmony *with* God, others, and the many webs of life. Once our eyes are open to the work of the Spirit in, through, and among us, our spiritual lives will demand new social, ecological, and economic behaviors.

Explore the TED Talk by Ray Anderson called "The Business Logic of Sustainability" at https://www.ted.com/talks/ray_anderson_on_the_business_logic_of_sustainability. What lessons did he teach? How did the creativity and ingenuity by those scaling Mount Sustainability reflect the creativity desired for us by the Spirit?

People of faith in Indonesia are reimagining new paths toward harmony. The current way companies are meeting the desire for palm oil and pulpwood is to burn down forests to make space for crops. This destroys the land and pollutes the air, causing serious harm to the people living on that land. Indonesia's highest Islamic authority saw the spiritual dimensions of this ecological problem and proclaimed that this practice is a sin, giving Muslims the spiritual courage to take a stand and imagine other ways to meet the needs of modern society.[1]

In 1997 the faith leader of the Eastern Orthodox Church, Patriarch Bartholomew, also spoke publicly about the spiritual gravity of ecological degradation. "For human beings to contaminate the earth's waters, land, air, and life—these are sins" (*LS* 8). Other faith leaders have also stepped up to protect our air. Listen to two remarks given by faith leaders at a 2014 EPA public hearing exploring carbon pollution from power plants.[2]

> An important question for Christians, and for all people of goodwill, is this: How much carbon pollution should power plants be permitted to dump into the atmosphere—for others to pay for in health, and in climate disruption costs? From the Evangelical and Reformed Christian perspective, it's clearly wrong for a buyer and a seller to enjoy all the benefits of a transaction, and then leave a substantial part of the cost for someone else to pick up—the external costs.
>
> John Elwood, New Jersey farmer and member of the Presbyterian Church

> I have been called by God to speak out on these issues, because it is my conviction as an Evangelical Christian that we must be stewards of God's creation. And, it seems abundantly clear to me that the EPA's carbon rule is a much-needed tool to carry out this call to be stewards of creation
>
> Reverend Richard Cizik, President, New Evangelical Partnership for the Common Good, Virginia

Reread the above quotes and then watch "Youth Climate Story: Air Pollution in Los Angeles," Our Climate Our Future: https://ourclimateourfuture.org/video/youth-climate-story-air-pollution-los-angeles/. How can you be a creation care leader in your church? What can you do to find out more about the levels of air pollution in your area and in other areas? How can your church help young parishioners be a faithful witness through active citizenship?

As elitist, destructive, and dysfunctional economic and political systems have become stronger, so has the resolve of faith leaders to give public witness to their faith in God who liberates. They continue to be inspired by the creative Spirit who has filled the universe with possibilities, and this has motivated their opposition to activities that put our atmospheres and people in jeopardy. Recently a group of Native Americans and more than five hundred clergy and Christian faith leaders from forty states delivered a letter to Interior Secretary Ryan Zinke opposing the weakening of the Methane and Waste Prevention Rule. To remain silent or blissfully ignorant to what is going on in the world was not an option for them. The following witness explains why:

> As people of faith, we have a moral obligation to care for our land, water, and air and to protect the health of our communities, and especially the children and future generations....Old Testament scripture states that before us have been set choices for life and death, "Choose life that you and your children might live." We appeal to you as an ethical leader to choose life by implementing the BLM methane rules as proposed.[3]

Rev. Susan Hendershot Guy, president of Interfaith Power & Light, also calls attention to how concerns for humans and Earth work together: "It is important to remember that frontline communities suffer the worst impacts of methane pollution, and people of faith are called to care for the most vulnerable in our society. At the same time, we know that this standard will not only address public health issues but create good paying jobs in communities that need them, along with royalties that will fund schools and local services."[4] These civic acts of creation care are prophetic acts of faith.

Pope Francis also witnesses to what he wrote in his encyclical. On August 1, 2018 he spoke to almost two dozen young men in formation for the priesthood, and when they asked how they can speak to the pain and depression often felt by young people today, he said, "Brothers, creativity is needed. A courageous creativity to find ways to act in that situation."[5] This courage is the fruit of an openness to the Spirit. His message of courageous creativity was not just for the ears of those young men. It was for all those seeking to live in this broken world and cultivate an intimate connection with the Spirit. Political and civic engagement informed and inspired by God's delight in the lilies of the field and care of the birds of the air (Matt 26:28–29) is not easy, nor is it a task for only a few. It is the task given to all of us and it will take every ounce of courage and creativity we can muster. We must remain vigilant, well informed, prayerful, and ecologically literate. We must forge authentic relationships with a diversity of people and be undeterred by the intolerance of others. Above all, we must not forget the message creation is trying to teach us: we are all caught up in a sacred, cosmic love story with so many beloved subjects connected through space and time. Hence, we are never alone in our witness to justice and peace in the skies above us.

DAILY AIR EXAMEN

Over four hundred years ago St. Ignatius of Loyola inspired people to a prayer-filled mindfulness via the Daily Examen. To conclude this section on air, let us prayerfully meditate on God's presence in our troubled blue skies using the Examen.

A) **Become aware of God's presence.** Reflect on your encounter with the mystery of air and the Holy Spirit in this chapter. The data, problems, Scripture, and passages from *Laudato Si'* may seem confusing to you—a blur, a jumble, a muddle. Ask God to bring clarity and understanding. Sit longer with areas where you felt God's voice speaking to you.

B) **Review the experience with gratitude.** Gratitude is the foundation of our relationship with God. Walk through your time exploring air in the presence of God and note its joys and delights. Focus on the gifts presented. Look at the wonder and power of air and breath within and around our inspirited bodies. See the work you did, the knowledge you learned, the inspirited bodies you interacted with. What did you receive from these encounters? What did you give in return? Pay attention to small things—God is in the details.

C) **Pay attention to your emotions.** One of St. Ignatius's great insights was that we detect the presence of the Spirit of God in the movements of our emotions. Reflect on the feelings you experienced during your encounter with air. Wonder? Awe? Elation? Resentment? Compassion? Anger? Mystery? Confidence? What is God saying through these feelings?

D) **God will most likely show you some ways that you fell short.** Make note of your areas of atmospheric illiteracy. What brokenness has resulted from your illiteracy. But look deeply for other implications. Does a feeling of frustration perhaps mean that the Holy Spirit wants you to consider a new direction in some area of your life? Are you concerned about a friend? About the children of tomorrow?

E) **Choose one feature of the day and pray from it.** Ask the Holy Spirit to direct you to something during your encounter with air and *Laudato Si'* that God thinks is particularly important. It may involve a feeling—positive or negative. It may be a significant encounter with another person, creature, or element, or a vivid moment of pleasure or peace. Or it may be something that seems rather insignificant. Look at it. Pray about it. Allow the prayer to arise spontaneously from your heart—whether intercession, praise, repentance, or gratitude.

F) **Look toward tomorrow.** Ask God to give you creativity and courage for tomorrow's challenges facing creation and humanity. What activities associated with the air could you do differently? Pay attention to the feelings that surface as you survey what's coming up. Are you doubtful? Cheerful? Apprehensive? Full of delighted anticipation? Allow these feelings to turn into prayer. Seek the Holy Spirit for guidance as you love air and our airborne neighbors, living every breath to the fullest. Ask God for help and understanding. Pray for hope.

St. Ignatius encouraged people to talk to Jesus like a friend, so conclude the Daily Examen with a conversation with *Jesus, incarnate*. Explore the ways Jesus guides how you develop an authentic relationship with air. Ask forgiveness for your sins stemming from illiteracy and apathy. Ask for his protection and inspiration. Ask for his wisdom about the questions you have and the problems facing creation, including yourself as part of this inspirited, breathless world. Do all this in the spirit of gratitude. Your life is a gift and expression of the Spirit's creativity and desire for justice. End your Examen by praying the Hail Mary, a prayer to the Mother blessed by the Holy Spirit to bear Jesus Christ.

IV

Fire

INTRODUCTION

> Were not our hearts burning within us while he was talking to us on the road, while he was opening the scriptures to us?
>
> Luke 24:32

The Greeks thought fire was one of the four basic building blocks of the universe. It was revered, feared, and the subjects of many myths. It was desired as a sacred substance and thought to give power to those who wield it. Take the story of Prometheus. He stole fire from the gods and gave it to humanity to ease their suffering and elevate them above the beasts. But modern science has taught us that fire is not really a "thing" but a process or series of interactive, energetic relationships. Fire is the result of a chemical reaction between the air, heat, and the flammable wick, and the product of these interactions (thermal energy) can be both life-giving and destructive. Yet the dancing flame of a candle is also entrancing and mysterious. When a candle is lit from another, the original flame never shrinks, and all are the same size, shape, and intensity as the first. Colorful flames dancing in a campfire, the molten coals, and the artistry of fireworks have mesmerized human minds for centuries—even before we knew them scientifically as combustion reactions. But our fascination should be tempered with fear because fire can also destroy habitats, homes, and lives. The bipolar nature of fire should constantly remind us that our mastery of creation is limited and fleeting. Nonetheless, fire can also ignite our appreciation of the energetic relationships of the Trinity and, in turn, it can teach us how to relate to other members of our planetary family.

Thus, this section invites readers to see fire as energy.[1] Faith leaders like those involved with the Pontifical Council for Justice and Peace (2014) and Christian ethicists like Christiana Peppard[2] have asked believers to reflect deeply on their relationship with the fuels that provide us with energy and make the changes that are urgently needed. Pope Francis agrees: "We know that technology based on the use of highly polluting fossil fuels—especially coal, but also oil and, to a lesser degree, gas—needs to be progressively replaced without delay" (*LS* 165). To do this we must hone our holy noticing. How is energy produced? How much do we use and why? What are the consequences of this use? To be stewards of creation, we must connect the dots. Energy use in our homes, workplaces, schools, and churches can be a faithful witness to God's invitation to love. Energy stewardship as love can offer new meaning previously hidden to the story of the burning bush.

> Read and reflect on Exodus 3:3–12. What does this passage tell us about the power of God? What could it tell us about nonrenewable energy sources? What justice aspects of this passage (e.g., freeing people from oppression) connect to energy injustices? Why is Moses's participation important? How could this motivate you to become "Moses"-like in our use of energy?

Notice that the bush was more than just a curiosity to lure Moses closer. Through this bush Moses noticed the sacredness of the ground and acted reverently. We, like Moses, walk on sacred ground given to us by God. Perhaps reimagining the story of the bush could help us to fall back in love with our common home and act reverently, doing whatever it takes to care for our planetary family, present and future. Interestingly, the bush was never consumed. Since God did not burn up the bush, maybe it is a sign that we should do likewise with fossil fuels.

A second way this biblical narrative can inform our energy stewardship is its message about injustice. God listened to the cries of the oppressed and speaks through the bush to name this injustice and work through Moses to liberate them. The cries of the poor and oppressed echo from unjust energy practices, as chapter 10 will demonstrate. God hears these cries, and like Moses, we are being challenged to go to Pharaoh and demand their release. Who is Pharaoh today? Today's pharaohs include large corporations, civic leaders, foundations, cultural norms, and politicians who create and nourish systems that promote fossil fuels and inhibit the emergence of new energy sources and social practices. However, the consumers of energy—you and I—are pharaohs too. Our insatiable demand and impatience make it profitable to blow up mountaintops, and extract oil from tar sands, shipping it through pipelines that leak into vulnerable ecosystems. Since God liberates, so should we.

Read the following statement from *Energy, Justice and Peace* by the Pontifical Council for Justice and Peace.

> Lack of access to energy results in income inequality and poverty, which in turn leads to global political instability and regional conflicts. Furthermore, exploitation of natural resources and the ways we produce and transport energy (oil, natural gas), degrade our planet, leading to food insecurity, habitat loss, poverty and more social unrest. However, thanks to technological ingenuity, political cooperation, forward thinking policies, and global awareness and concern, energy is becoming a strategic element moving us towards the solutions to many social and ecological problems.[3]

What do you think? How often have you connected your energy use with your faith life? How could reflections on energy become a bigger part of your prayer life and daily activities?

The wisdom offered in *Laudato Si'* about the Trinity can guide our path to authentic energy stewardship. This is the subject of chapter 11 and builds upon what was offered already on the Holy Spirit. Chapter 12 offers concrete examples of how energy stewardship can ignite a reader's passion for peace and justice.

Chapter 10

ALL FIRED UP

What Are We Doing to Power Our Ecological Crisis?

> We are the beneficiaries of two centuries of enormous change.... Technology has remedied countless evils which used to harm and limit human beings. How can we not feel gratitude and appreciation for this progress?
>
> *Laudato Si'* 101

Through the ages, fire and other energy sources have changed how we relate to each other and with the planet. When wood was burned for heat, light, and cooking, living conditions improved, people took more time to socialize, and vibrant cultural practices were born. When oxen provided us the pulling power to till the soil, agriculture emerged, and this more stationary life changed how humans lived together. When the energy from flowing streams was harnessed, gristmills arose, changing what we ate and how we could tell who was rich (white bread) and who was not (dark bread). When the power of steam was captured, mechanized weaving looms emerged, and this changed how we appreciated artists. It also paved the way to our current reliance on machines and an industrial way of life. Thus, a turn to industrial living also meant we needed more abundant and powerful energy sources. When forests in Europe became depleted, people began looking across the seas for wood to burn. They also looked deep into the Earth for new deposits of a powerful energy source discovered centuries before: coal. We also discovered electricity, natural gas, and nuclear energy to power our world.

SOURCES OF ENERGY

Coal is a black rock made from dead plant matter in swampy areas that was pressed together under tremendous pressure over hundreds of millions of years. It is a nonrenewable fossil fuel because it takes an exceptionally long time to make the lump of fossilized carbon, and when it is gone, we will have to wait hundreds of millions of years for more. And only if the conditions are exactly right for this process. Over the last few centuries, other fossil fuels have been discovered to feed our industrial and technological lifestyles: crude oil, petroleum, and natural gas. All these need to be extracted from our planet, are nonrenewable, and incur high human and ecological costs for their use.

Our discovery and use of coal and fossil fuels has impacted all aspects of human life. The asphalt roads we drive on are a product of refined crude oil. Our car tires are synthetic rubber made from petroleum and gas (refined crude oil) fuels the engines in our vehicles. These innovations have changed society, especially our shopping habits and expectations. This change can be both good (e.g., improved health and time savings) and bad (e.g., an amnesia concerning natural limits and the reasons for them). We need to notice both. If your feet are cold and you want to avoid getting sick, you can easily (and quickly) buy several pairs of socks rather than undertaking the longer process of knitting a pair from the wool collected from the local sheep farmer. Today, a family from Toronto can have fresh, healthy strawberries in March rather than having to do without or relying on preserved berries they would have harvested in the spring. The transportation systems that give us these options rely on fossil fuels. They also enable us to live far away from where we go to school, church, or work. We can meet and fall in love with people on different continents, and buses and trains allow us to organize communities in ways undreamed of prior to fossil fuels. How we relax has also changed. Beaches in Maui are accessible to North Carolinians at any time thanks to airplanes fueled by 36,000 gallons (150,000 L)[1] of refined crude oil. We can also put some steaks on a barbeque fueled by another form of refined crude oil (propane) and be entertained when we click on our TVs powered by electricity.

The U.S. Energy Information Administration claims that in 2017 approximately 4,015 billion kilowatt hours (kWh) of electricity was generated for human use and about 83 percent was from nonrenewable energy sources (63 percent fossil fuels, 20 percent nuclear energy).[2] Some of this electricity has vastly improved our quality of life and some has not. But possessing this energy has changed how we live, move, and have our being on Earth. Every room in your home, classroom, parish, and workspace has electrical outlets, but how often do we think about the source of that electricity or how it got there or the cost to people and the planet? Like water, we do not even notice energy until we lose it. Hurricanes Maria and Florence taught us that without power, millions have no way to cool themselves, pump water, refrigerate food, or flush toilets. Schooling, health care, and businesses were all disrupted, and lives were lost. Thus, extractive, nonrenewable energy sources are omnipresent and have transformed human life. However, we cannot ignore the grave costs incurred when we extract and use them.

Calculate your carbon footprint at https://www.nature.org/en-us/get-involved/how-to-help/carbon-footprint-calculator/. How do you score compared to the average? Did anything surprise you? In what areas could you be a more faithful energy steward?

THE COST OF OUR ENERGETIC LIFESTYLES

When coal is taken out of the ground, it produces many toxic by-products (sulfur and coal dust). Coal dust is harmful to lungs and when the sulfur mixes with the water in the air, sulfuric acid is formed and rains down on Earth, causing problems for buildings and bodies. Some coal deposits are accessed by blowing the tops off mountains, and this process destroys habitats, pollutes drinking water, and leads to health problems in nearby communities.[3] Fracking is when natural gas is released from deep underground, but it requires the injection of toxic chemicals into the ground to force the gas out.[4] Crude oil below Earth's surface is drawn up by oil wells and transported over long distances (pipelines or shipping vessels) for processing and use. Our methods of transporting crude oil can devastate local ecosystems when they leak due to explosions (2010 Deep Water Horizon—210 million gallons spilled) or low pressure (2017 Keystone Pipeline—200,000 gallons) or when tankers run a ground (1989 Exxon Valdez—11 million gallons spilled) or when used as a war tactic (1991 Gulf War—240 million gallons intentionally spilled). Extracting crude oil from tar sands requires the clearing of ground vegetation, destroying the habitats for both humans and animals. The rapid industrial development in the Athabasca oil sands region of Alberta, Canada, is a vivid reminder of the high cost of this extraction process. Environmental impact studies have shown that harmful materials are polluting the soil, water, air, and our food. Thus, "future risk to humans and wildlife because of surface mining activity in the Athabasca oil sands region has been underestimated."[5] Nuclear power plants seem to be cleaner, but when the radioactive waste is considered, this is not a wise option. It is costly and risky to safely dispose of radioactive materials anywhere on our planet. The vulnerable among us will suffer more if we choose this route—as the tragedy at the Love Canal showed us.[6] The Love Canal in Niagara Falls was the site used by a chemical company to house its toxic waste, and a community was built on it, thinking it was safe. Sadly, residents of the Love Canal did not know how very wrong this assumption was. God, the Liberator of the oppressed, hears the cries of the oppressed, and so should we. Finding nonextractive, less "dirty," more sustainable energy sources is a prophetic act of faith.

When we burn fossil fuels another significant problem arises. The carbon trapped for millions of years is released into the atmosphere as carbon dioxide, an air pollutant described in chapter 9. Trapping coal deposits in the Earth has helped keep the planet's climate system in a fluid harmony, and our releasing of this huge storehouse of carbon into the air over the last 250 years has put this balance in jeopardy. Science has shown that the amount of carbon dioxide in the atmosphere has significantly increased since the preindustrial era, thanks mostly to fossil fuel use. A major effect of these high amounts is the warming of our planet (as stated in the other sections). Prediction models made by the IPCC show that by 2100, even if we try our best to curb our fossil fuel use, Earth's temperature will have risen about 1.5 degrees. This does not seem like much, but we are already feeling the effects with more unpredictable and intense storms and weather systems around the world. Hurricanes are more frequent and fiercer, and droughts and cold periods are longer, more common, and more intense.[7] The IPCC's Fifth World Assessment Report states that there are considerable risks associated with the changes in climate we are seeing, and this is at only 1 or 2°C above preindustrial levels. If the temperature rises even more, the effects intensify exponentially. We need to diminish our dependency on nonrenewable, polluting fossil fuels and be more faithful energy stewards, for Earth's sake.

> Watch the following video by the Intergovernmental Panel on Climate Change (IPCC), "Climate Change 2013: The Physical Science Basis," Nov. 21, 2013, at https://www.youtube.com/watch?v=6yiTZm0y1YA. What did you see or hear that helped you understand how climate change is a global phenomenon? How does this video affirm that it will take a "village" to address this situation? As people of faith, what could you or your church do to help?

Pope Francis joins the voices of scientists across the globe warning of our unsustainable reliance on nonrenewable energy sources, and he names energy as a common good we should pursue wisely:

> The fact is that "contemporary man has not been trained to use power well," because our immense technological development has not been accompanied by a development in human responsibility, values, and conscience....The risk is growing day by day that man will not use his power as he should. (*LS* 105)

Energy that powers our technological lifestyles is valuable for bringing forth abundant life *only* when the four cardinal virtues—prudence, fortitude, temperance, and justice—guide us. Prudence requires that we acknowledge the costs associated with our extraction and use of nonrenewable, dirty energy sources, and temperance demands us to be more moderate in our energy use. Without courage, inspired by justice and love, we will not make the necessary changes in our behaviors and discover more life-giving energy options. This is how *Laudato Si'* calls people of faith to be energy stewards. The next chapter will offer the theological wisdom of *Laudato Si'* to guide our transformation from being the "most irresponsible" people to those who joyfully "shoulder [our] grave responsibility" to care for our common home as faithful energy stewards (*LS* 165).

Chapter 11

WISDOM FROM *LAUDATO SI'* TO GUIDE US

> The natural environment is a collective good...and the responsibility of everyone....That is why the New Zealand bishops asked what the commandment "Thou shall not kill" means when "twenty percent of the world's population consumes resources at a rate that robs the poor nations and future generations of what they need to survive."
>
> *Laudato Si'* 95

Throughout *Laudato Si'*, Pope Francis presents the triune family as a model for integral ecology and human flourishing. But how can we know an infinite God? Pope Francis claims that we can know something of the Creator when we recover and respect the "rhythms inscribed in nature by the hand of the Creator" (*LS* 71). In a chapter called "The Gospel of Creation," Pope Francis highlights how each aspect of creation participates in a harmonious world created by God: "We can say that 'alongside revelation properly so-called, contained in sacred Scripture, there is a divine manifestation in the blaze of the sun and the fall of night.'" When we pay attention to God's self-communication in the world, we will "learn to see ourselves in relation to all other creatures" (*LS* 85). Humanity is part of the web of life on our sacred planet: "all of us are linked by unseen bonds and together form a kind of universal family, a sublime communion which fills us with a sacred, affectionate and humble respect" (*LS* 89). Everything in the universe is connected and this reflects the triune communion of love that created it. We must take up our vocation of being creative energy stewards; otherwise our planetary family will be harmed further. "Concern for the environment thus needs to be joined to a sincere love for our fellow human beings and an unwavering commitment to resolving the problems of society" (*LS* 91). We can live more harmoniously with creation when we contemplate the source of it all: the Trinity.

GOD AS TRINITY

Pope Francis makes the clear connection between the relationality of the Trinity and our relations on Earth: "The divine Persons are subsistent relations, and the world created according to the divine model, is a web of relationships" (*LS* 240). God the Creator is the ultimate source of everything, the Son intimately united himself with Earth, and the Spirit is the creative dynamism and bond of love at the heart of the universe (*LS* 238). They are a perfect communion—they have perfected "being with" one another.

> I once read something along the lines of this: "How many Friday night fish fries, Saturday afternoon BBQ's, and game nights did Jesus have with his disciples before he popped the question 'Who do you say I am?'" For Jesus, it is about belonging together and talking to each other first and believing second. We need to learn to be *with* people, to live life in communion with those around us. Jesus did not just go out and invite people to church, he "did" life with them and showed them church. In life, it is easy to take the position of a teacher above others, where we believe that we know more than others, and this can lead to a monologue. If we take the position of a student, where we view each relationship as an opportunity to learn from another, a dialogue begins. When dialogues begin, lives change.
> (Tripp Wright, graduate student in a masters in global services program at Abilene Christian University, excerpt from an introductory reflection, September 2018)

We exist because of the webs of ecological, social, and spiritual relationships, not independent of them. "When we contemplate with wonder the universe in all its grandeur and beauty, we must praise the whole Trinity" (*LS* 238). The Trinity has left its mark on creation if we would only notice. Holy noticing will inspire us to strive for creative, empowering relations of love in our planetary communion that enable abundant life for all because this is what the divine triune family does. We need to learn to "be with" one another better. We need to get to know our neighbors better: who they are, what their gifts are, and what enables them to have abundant life. When we awaken to how interdependent we are with our neighbors and how we create life and love together, then the development and use of renewable energy sources—wind, solar, geothermal, and hydropower—and the embracing of less energy-intensive lifestyles are faithful expressions of our love of God.

> Creatures tend toward God, and in turn it is proper to every living being to tend toward other things, so that throughout the universe we can find any number of constant and secretly interwoven relationships. This leads us not only to marvel at the manifold connections existing among creatures, but also to discover a key to our own fulfillment. The human person grows more, matures more and is sanctified more to the extent that he or she enters into relationships, going out of themselves to live in communion with God, with others and with all creatures. In this way, they make their own the trinitarian dynamism which God imprinted in them when they were created. (*LS* 240)

A green energy path will allow us all to reach our fullest potential as images of a Triune God: Lover, Beloved, and Love.

> After reading the above quote from *Laudato Si'*, watch the trailer for the HBO documentary *Happening: A Clean Energy Revolution* (https://www.youtube.com/watch?v=JwfdfNRcpAo). With what types of energy are you familiar? What ones were new and worth looking into? In what ways could your church be part of this revolution?

We may think faithful energy stewardship just means driving less or having fewer gas-guzzling cars, but as discussed in chapter 1, the production of plastics requires a lot of water and fossil fuels. Thus, we need to both drive less and buy more wisely—as well as other life choices. This does not have to be a hardship; stewardship of creation can be a joyful response to the gospel. Today we are invited to build strong webs of love between lovers and beloveds that will not tolerate anything less than abundant life for all. It requires truth seeking, ingenuity, integrity, perseverance, and creativity to continually orient our actions toward Love. The next section explores stories of some faithful energy stewards who are radiating trinitarian dynamism and inspiring others to love our common home in creative ways.

Chapter 12

LIVING *LAUDATO SI'*

How to Care for Our Common Home

> Many things have to change course, but it is we human beings above all who need to change. We lack an awareness of our common origin, of our mutual belonging, and of a future to be shared with everyone. This basic awareness would enable the development of new convictions, attitudes, and forms of life. A great cultural, spiritual, and educational challenge stands before us, and it will demand that we set out on the long path of renewal.
>
> *Laudato Si'* 202

A retired teacher recently recounted the thrill of discovery his students experienced when they all held hands and were able to light up an energy ball. Each student was a necessary part of a living circuit, where electricity passed from body to body until it finally reached the ball and its light shone brightly as it detected the dancing electrons. If anybody let go, the circuit would have been broken and the light would have remained dark. All were needed to harness the energy flowing through Earth's life systems, and like that human circuit, we are all needed to transform darkness into light. There are many dynamic energy stewards, from political and church leaders to family members in the pews. Here are just a few hopeful stories to stoke the embers of your imaginations.

Pope Francis laments the weak response of leaders to climate change and other ecological and social crises: "These situations have caused sister earth, along with all the abandoned of our world, to cry out, pleading that we take another course....The problem is that we still lack the culture needed to confront this crisis. We lack leadership capable of striking out on new paths and meeting the needs of the present with concern for all and without prejudice toward coming generations" (*LS* 53). Recognizing his own personal responsibility to lead, in 2018 he used his political, spiritual, and social power and privilege as pope to call a gathering of the leaders of energy companies, like Exxon and BP, to urge the development of renewable energies. "There is no time to lose" he told them.[1] He then met with entrepreneurs and leaders in business on September 1, the World Day of Prayer for Care of Creation,[2] to challenge them and point their creativity energies toward clean energy.

> Reflect on Matthew 18:20 and then watch a news clip of Pope Francis meeting with energy executives and Catholic leaders: "Pope Warns Energy Bosses of Global Destruction," Reuters, June 9, 2018, https://www.reuters.com/video/watch/pope-warns-energy-bosses-of-global-destr-id434393087. What do you think could come of this gathering? Read paragraphs 213 and 214 in *Laudato Si'*. How do these passages move you to action? In what ways could you, your family, and your church be energy stewards?

Academic leaders and teachers are also using their position and privilege to become energy stewards within their professional lives. For example, Dr. Laurie Zoloth, the 2014 president of the American Academy of Religion (AAR), deliberately chose climate change as the central theme of the academy's annual conference. This decision mobilized the considerable talents of tens of thousands of academics and teachers for the expressed purpose of examining climate change. Her reason was provocative: "I decided it was the core moral issue of our time....And I had one chance to really say I don't know the answer—we don't know the answer, and we're faced with this. The scientists on my campus are frantic about this science. Every scientific panel I went to was filled with incredibly anxious scientists." She mentioned that they kept asking about her religion colleagues and what they were doing about climate change.[3] She decided to find out and challenged religion scholars across the globe to make climate change the focus of their work. The result was a diverse range of presentations and papers—from an exploration of Zen Buddhist Oxherding Pictures, to Climate Change and the Apocalyptic Imagination, to Ecofeminism and Earth Healing.[4] One of the keynote speakers was a scientist and former leader of the Intergovernmental Panel on Climate Change (IPCC). He spoke of the power of religion to offer different ways of looking at the world and alternative value systems that could help address the current ecological crises and promote justice. Religion has the power to change people's hearts, something science is not built to do.

Catholic churches, other religious institutions, and Christian missionaries have also embraced their responsibility to be good energy stewards, and they have guidance from groups such as Green Faith, Catholic Climate Covenant, Interfaith Power and Light, the Global Catholic Climate Movement, and SonLight Power. They demonstrate this stewardship in many ways: through environmental leadership programs, creation-centered prayer life, the implementing of energy-efficient practices and policies, the promotion of energy conservation, energy efficiency, and renewable energy, and the use of solar power to share God's love.

> Watch this video: "SonLight Power: Our Story in Action," Sept. 29, 2014 at https://www.youtube.com/watch?time_continue=5&v=CWvsIq_8624. How does this video stretch your vision of what Christian missions means, both in the United States and further afield? How has your vision of God's love expanded?

On October 4, 2015, at the Feast of St. Francis, many religious organizations placed their money where their hearts were, announcing they would not invest money in groups involved with nonrenewable, dirty energy from extraction of fossil fuels, to fracking operations, to coal mining.[5] This divestment movement is gaining ground, with over three thousand UK churches having switched to green energy (or planning to),[6] over fifteen thousand mosques in Morocco having green makeovers by March 2019,[7] and the Anglican Church of Southern Africa's voting to divest from fossil fuels in 2016.[8] Fossil-free investing makes moral and financial sense, but it also means that companies that have smaller carbon footprints and develop renewable energies will get financial and social support, better technologies will get to market faster, and carbon emissions will diminish. Shareholders and stock owners need to notice where their money is being invested and how it shows what they are valuing. This is made a little easier by search platforms like Fossil Free Funds[9] that allow you to match your investing with your values.[10] Some argue that green products always cost more but this is a myth. Companies would make more green products if more people bought them, and if more people refused to buy anything else, they would cost much less and the new economic avenues and jobs could be created. Also, when all costs (e.g., coal ash cleanup, rebuilding ecosystems, treating chronic diseases) are factored in, products that are responsibly sourced and produced are, in fact, much cheaper.

Faith communities are also designing sacred worship spaces in ways that promote energy stewardship: rooftop solar panels and gardens, energy-efficient lights, efficient air conditioning and heating units (that they use less), window placement that reflects heat in the summer and absorbs it in the winter, underground parking to heat the pews above, and provocative sermons and catecheses that connect the sacred space in and out of the church with the Scripture and rituals. Examples of green sacred spaces were highlighted in chapter 6 (e.g., St. Gabriel's parish, the Sisters of St. Joseph Motherhouse in Toronto, Dominican Sister's Genesis Farm), but an example of direct energy stewardship is the solar panel initiatives at St. Eugene's parish in Asheville, North Carolina. They have saved more than $13,800 in electricity costs in two years and taught about the love of God, self, and neighbor through conservation of energy. Energy stewardship in the design of sacred spaces intertwines practice, worship, and doctrine, and this is how we learn to stir our embers for justice carried in our hearts into a roaring, transformative fire.

Pope Francis also highlights the family as "the place in which life—the gift of God—can be properly welcomed and protected" (*LS* 213), because it is the first place we learn how to love. Thus, families and individuals can show great love for creation in the same way institutions do. Every dollar invested or spent can be a statement of what you value and a lesson on how to love. Years ago, a wise Catholic nun spoke to senior administrators at a Catholic board of education in Ontario, Canada, and she said something I will never forget—and often repeat: if you want to know the mission of a school board, religious organization, or business, don't look at the mission statement, look at the budget. Whatever you value is where you will put your money. Pope Francis, quoting Benedict XVI, agrees: "Purchasing is always a moral—and not simply economic—act" (*LS* 206). Families can champion the energy stewardship by avoiding (or moderately) spending their money on things that support companies using nonrenewable energy sources or in the fossil fuel industry itself. This means that we will have to humbly notice the impact of our actions as individuals and families, and learn more about energy sources, how things are made, and what companies promote a green covenant. Cardinal Peter Turkson echoes how important families are to the process of caring for creation: "Social pressure—including from boycotting certain products—can force businesses to consider their environmental footprint and patterns of production."[11] If we consume less and value renewable energy or processes more, we are being faithful energy stewards. We also need to ask ourselves if we need so much stuff. Perhaps the virtue of temperance can be shown by not shopping. This is just as prophetic an act as buying green products. Being an energy steward—shopping wisely and more moderately—means sacrifice and change in our expectations and habits. But many families are holy noticing and embracing energy efficiency because energy use has dropped 1.1 percent in the United States since 2008, and battery-powered energy storage has grown seventeenfold since 2008. Annual sales of electric vehicles have grown to 104,000, but consumers will still have to be prudent and investigate how the electricity powering their cars is being produced. Thus, being an energy steward can begin at home.[12]

In the book *Walmart Effect*, it was noted that sales at Walmart far exceeded increases in populations. They concluded that "people just had more underwear stored in their house than they really needed or had had in the past."[13] Underwear was so cheap and so irresistibly displayed, people bought it even if they did not need it. Take stock of your closets and drawers. Discuss how susceptible we are to impulse shopping. How could we be wiser in our shopping habits? How does Pope Francis help us understand temperance (moderation) in how we shop and consume?

Laudato Si' explains that another personal act of love in the form of energy stewardship occurs in the civic and political realms (*LS* 228–32). On May 24, 2019, there were thousands of climate strikes around the world organized by the Global Catholic Climate Movement. Bishops from Argentina and Trinidad and Tobago, and other Catholic lay leaders, took part in the prophetic protest. Choosing who should hold public office and policy development can also be a manifestation of creation care. Energy stewards in California have recently taken a bold step. On August 30, 2018, elected state officials passed landmark legislation committing California to 100 percent renewable and zero-carbon energy sources by 2045. This commitment, and others, will fire up local and national economies as people put their talents and time toward more renewable energy in the form of wind, solar, geothermal, and other noncarbon-based, renewable energies. Recently, in San Francisco, political, scientific, and church leaders from around the world gathered for the Global Climate Action Summit (September 12–14, 2018).[14] It was a time to celebrate the achievements of states, cities, companies, investors, and citizens in addressing climate change and launch new, deeper commitments and faster climate action. At this summit, Global Catholic Climate Movement hosted an event called "Living *Laudato Si'* through Climate Action" to announce the latest number of signatories on the Catholic Climate Declaration and showcase parishes, dioceses, religious orders, organizations, ministries, and institutions that are caring for our planet by reducing their use of fossil fuels. They also celebrated the deep love of human neighbors shown by people's commitment to justice. An example was when people protested the prioritization of profits from the Dakota Pipeline that was outweighing the rights of local Sioux to clean water.

Read the following action taken in July 2018 by religious congregation the Adorers of the Blood of Christ in Columbia, Pennsylvania, who protested the building of a pipeline on their property: Catholic News Service, "Sisters Mark Anniversary of Cornfield Chapel Symbolizing Pipeline Protest," July 10, 2018, https://www.globalsistersreport.org/news/environment/sisters-mark-anniversary-cornfield-chapel-symbolizing-pipeline-protest-54941. Begin a conversation about the role protest has in the lives of biblical and contemporary prophets.

Leaders in the United Church of Christ also offer an example of energy stewardship in their call to action:

> As Christians, we, the undersigned clergy, are conditioned by the gospel to stand on the side of the persecuted and the jailed. As such, we are compelled by our faith to stand with the water protectors of Standing Rock, who have

pricked the conscience of a nation and the world. In opposing the Dakota Access Pipeline that would carry oil from North Dakota to Illinois, they have resolutely declared that they are not protestors but protectors and defenders acting out of a sacred obligation which affirms "water is life."[15]

Others like the National Council of Churches and the Creation Justice Ministries applaud this conversion to justice for "as Christians, we have a moral responsibility to stand with indigenous peoples to protect their sovereignty, and God's creation."[16] The personal acts of solidarity made by many Christians and church leaders to stand alongside the water protectors at Standing Rock was a prophetic form of creation care.

These individual, familial, ecclesial, and political acts of energy stewardship are deeply faithful to the Gospel call to love. Big and small, private and public acts done with great love are how we will build the kind of world God wants for us all.

DAILY FIRE EXAMEN

Over four hundred years ago, St. Ignatius of Loyola inspired people to a prayer-filled mindfulness via the Daily Examen. To conclude this section on fire, let us prayerfully meditate on God's presence and energy literacy using the Examen.

A) **Become aware of God's presence.** Reflect on your encounter with the mystery and power of fire in this chapter in the company of the Holy Spirit. The data, problems, Scripture, and passages from *Laudato Si'* may seem confusing to you—a blur, a jumble, a muddle. Ask God to bring clarity and understanding. Sit longer with areas where you felt God's voice speaking to you.

B) **Review the experience with gratitude.** Gratitude is the foundation of our relationship with God. Walk through your time exploring fire in the presence of God and note its joys and delights. Focus on the gifts presented. Look at the wonderful and awful power of fire. See the work you did, the knowledge you learned, the people you interacted with. What did you receive from these encounters? What did you give in return? Pay attention to small things—God is in the details.

C) **Pay attention to your emotions.** One of St. Ignatius's great insights was that we detect the presence of the Spirit of God in the movements of our emotions. Reflect on the feelings you experienced during your encounter with fire. Wonder? Awe? Elation? Resentment? Compassion? Anger? Mystery? Confidence? What is God saying through these feelings?

D) **God will most likely show you some ways that you fell short.** Make note of your areas of energy illiteracy. What brokenness has resulted from your illiteracy? But look deeply for other implications. Does a feeling of frustration perhaps mean that God wants you to consider a new direction in some area of your life? Are you concerned about a friend? About the children of tomorrow?

E) **Choose one feature of the day and pray from it.** Ask the Holy Spirit to direct you to something during your encounter with fire and *Laudato Si'* that God thinks is particularly important. It may involve a feeling—positive or negative. It may be a significant encounter with another person, creature, or element, or a vivid moment of pleasure or peace. Or it may be something that seems rather insignificant. Look at it. Pray about it. Allow the prayer to arise spontaneously from your heart—whether intercession, praise, repentance, or gratitude.

F) **Look toward tomorrow.** Ask God to give you passion and humility for tomorrow's challenges facing creation and humanity. What activity involving fire or energy could you do differently? Pay attention to the feelings that surface as you survey what's coming up. Are you doubtful? Cheerful? Apprehensive? Full of delighted anticipation? Allow these feelings to turn into prayer. Seek your Creator for guidance as you love and live with fire anew. Ask God for help and understanding. Pray for hope.

St. Ignatius encouraged people to talk to Jesus like a friend, so conclude the Daily Examen with a conversation with *Jesus, second person of the Trinity*. Explore the ways Jesus guides how you develop an authentic relationship with fire. Ask forgiveness for your sins stemming from your energy illiteracy and apathy. Ask for his protection and inspiration. Ask for his wisdom about the questions you have and the problems facing creation, including yourself as part of this dynamic, energetic world. Do all this in the spirit of gratitude. Your life is a gift and expression of fire's creativity and blessedness. End your Examen by praying the Glory Be to the Father.

CONCLUSION

> We need a new and universal solidarity...."Everyone's talents and involvement are needed to redress the damage caused by human abuse of God's creation." All of us can cooperate as instruments of God for the care of creation, each according to his or her own culture, experience, involvements and talents.
>
> *Laudato Si'* 14

Water, Earth, air, and fire—four aspects of our planetary home and places of divine revelation. Our sacred waters, soil, air, and energetic relations are places of great distress and this is compounding the suffering of the poor. They are also sources of great wisdom to encourage prophetic acts of great love. In every community, people of faith are showing that they are not overwhelmed and paralyzed by the gravity of Earth's problems. They are *noticing* the grave consequences of how we are living and loving today and are *on fire* via the Spirit to *create* a better world.

What this book tries to do is not only to *talk about* ecological conversion and integral ecology; rather it is designed for people in the pews, porches, parish halls, and pulpits *to be engaged in holy noticing* and become *living witnesses* to a "commitment to creation set before us by the Gospel of Jesus" (*LS* 246).

I find that it is easy to reduce the ecological crises to the corruption of political leaders and the greed of corporations. True, divisive political rhetoric is used to maintain the status quo for the powerful, even when it is detrimental to so many. However, blaming a faceless government or corporation is too simple and diminishes personal responsibility. The purpose of corporations and governments is to *serve the people*. The legitimacy of their position is created and sustained by the people. People should hold them accountable in a democratic society and value a viable home for their grandchildren more than the maintenance of political affiliations and status. In my life this means opening myself and becoming vulnerable to others. It means spending time with my nephew and cousins every chance I get. It means having respectful conversations with people who have radically different opinions than I do. It means realizing that being right does not matter if I have made others feel less than human. It means appreciating that prisoners and anyone who counts as the "least of these" are human beings with inherent dignity and just because they are out of sight does not mean they should be out of mind. It means realizing that places I dwell and people I talk to have something of value that I need to experience. It means empowering those who have been disempowered to be their own liberators—and cheering them on as they do. Ultimately, addressing the problems of the world means practicing what you preach and loving yourself, others, and all of creation along the way.

Excerpt from a conversation in 2018 with C. J. James, religion and psychology graduate student at Wake Forest University

As a small Lenten reading group, homilist, workshop leader, or individual, dive deeply into the data, narratives, quizzes, reflections, discussions, and Daily Examens and let yourself experience God's presence in our wonderful and fragile world. Practice your holy noticing so when you put down this book, the skill stays with you and you see God working through you, others, and the natural world to bring life from death. Do not despair; the story of the nativity, our Christian ancestors, and Pope Francis continually remind us that God is with us and has not abandoned us. We have many lampposts to light our way and ignite our spirits. Where are these lampposts today? There are many if you look with eyes of faith: a neighbor who chose imperfect produce; a roommate who took a shorter shower; a nonprofit that planted a community garden; a couple planning a green wedding or funeral; a vacationing family who turned off their beachfront condo's lights at night to help birds navigate; a youth minister who taught young adults to track air pollution; a priest who included his church's energy consumption in a sermon; a grandmother who prayed daily for Earth's many subjects. These are prophetic acts of love witnessing to God, the Lord of life.

If we love God with every ounce of our being and our planetary neighbors as ourselves, then we must live in harmony with creation. St. Francis is a perfect example: he loved God with abandon and sought abundant life for all his brothers and sisters. God is reflected in all that exists, and to worship God we must live in harmony and solidarity with Brother Sun, Sister Moon and stars, Brother Wind, Sister Water, and Brother Fire. Pope Francis has let this lesson guide him and so should we. When we truly fall in love with the wonderful and often perplexing world and join with all our fellow pilgrims on this journey, we will realize in our bones that we are part of an immense cosmic family. We will remember who and whose we are. And this rootedness and belonging will bring great peace and joy. "In union with all creatures, we journey through this land seeking God.... Let us sing as we go. May our struggles and our concern for this planet never take away the joy of our hope" (*LS* 244).

Laudato Si'
Praise Be.

INTERACTIVE ACTIVITIES AND DISCUSSION QUESTIONS FOR CHAPTERS 1–3

WHAT DO YOU KNOW ABOUT WATER?

Instructions: Sign up for a free quizlet account at https://quizlet.com. Search for the quizlet titled "What Do You Know about Water" by WU religion alumni Mary Katherine Williams (mkwilliams98). Then take the following quiz to see how water literate you are. You can choose from eight different ways to interact with the materials. Take a test to see what you know or use flashcards to learn more or really test yourself via the timed matching game. Afterward, reflect individually or as a group on the following questions:

1. Was there anything that surprised you? How literate do you feel about water?
2. What about water could you celebrate more? Are there any aspects about water that concern you?
3. How could this knowledge impact how you appreciate and use water in your everyday life and in your faith life?

CHAPTERS 1–3 REFLECTION AND DISCUSSION QUESTIONS

1. Meditate on the part water plays in the Genesis Creation stories (chaps. 1 and 2), Exodus (17:1–7), and the Psalms (104:10–13). Does your new appreciation for the limited nature of drinkable water and the connection of water and energy impact how you understand the depth of meaning in these Bible passages?
2. How can water illiteracy and water poverty lead to a deficiency in how we understand the Creator, Jesus as living water, divine revelation, and salvation,

as seen in Isaiah 12:3; 43:16–21? What does Ezekiel 34:18 teach us about limits to our water use?

3. Reflect on paragraphs 27–31 and 211–13 of *Laudato Si'*, then watch any or all of the following from The Story of Stuff Project: "The Story of Bottled Water" (https://storyofstuff.org/movies/story-of-bottled-water/); "Let's Ban the Bead!" (https://storyofstuff.org/movies/lets-ban-the-bead/); "The Story of Microfibers" (https://storyofstuff.org/movies/story-of-microfibers/); and "A Tale of Two Cities" (Flint and Evart, Michigan) (https://storyofstuff.org/movies/tale-of-two-cities/). How does water poverty manifest in the films? How do these videos impact your understanding of Matthew 22:36–40 and the passages from *Laudato Si'*? What new water behaviors could you employ in your family, church, business, or school?
4. Learn about Imperfect Produce at www.imperfectproduce.com and then reflect on the scriptural narrative of the rich young man (Matt 19:16–30; Mark 10:17–31; Luke 18:18–30). What message from Scripture speaks to you in light of what you have learned about food and water waste? How does "sell all you possess and give to the poor" take on new meaning considering water poverty and our throwaway culture?
5. Reflect on the words of Luna Leopold: "Water is the most critical resource issue of our lifetime and our children's lifetime. The health of our waters is the principle measure of how we live on the land." Research the following three items: November 2017 Keystone pipeline leak (210,000 gallons) in South Dakota; the contamination of wells by fracking operations in Pavillion, Wyoming; the Standing Rock occupation at Lake Oahe that was protesting a new pipeline that would threaten the Sioux tribe's drinking water. How well are we living on the land? Would you move your family to live beside an oil pipeline or fracking operation? Should others have to live there? What does *Laudato Si'* say about these activities? Explore and discuss available alternative energies and less energy intensive lifestyles.
6. How do worship songs capture the sacredness of Earth's watery depths and inform your understanding of God as Mystery? Listen to your favorite hymns that involve water. How do all the creatures of the sea recognize God, Creator and respond to love with love? How is the intrinsic worth of all creatures of the sea expressed? How should hymns inform humans' activities?
7. How do you think your local faith leaders understand the spiritual significance of water and water stewardship? Watch the following short film on local watersheds and faith created by Keeping Watch (UNC Charlotte College of Arts and Architecture and UNC Charlotte Urban Institute): http://keepingwatch.org/programming/creeks/stewardship. How does this resonate what was offered by Pope Francis in *Laudato Si'*?

8. Meditate on the following passage from *Laudato Si'*: "All of us can cooperate as instruments of God for the care of creation, each according to his or her own culture, experience, involvements and talents." (*LS* 14). What are your gifts? Where can you make positive actions to counter water poverty? What challenges may you face? How will you articulate the benefits of this new way of living and loving?
9. Explore the parable of the river: Imagine a large river with a high waterfall. At the bottom of this waterfall hundreds of people are working frantically to rescue those who have fallen into the river. One individual looks up and sees a seemingly never-ending stream of people cascading down the waterfall, and he begins to run upstream. One of his fellow rescuers hollers, "Where are you going? There are so many people that need help here." The man replied, "I'm going upstream to find out why so many people are falling into the river" (attributed to the 1930s social reformer Saul Alinksy). Discuss the following: What downstream work do you or your church/school do (e.g., food, money, clothing donations)? What upstream work do you do (e.g., changing political, environmental, or cultural policies that impact the poor)? How could you balance these two approaches to social justice?
10. At his weekly general audience in St. Peter's Square on August 29, 2018, Pope Francis called for "concrete action to combat the 'emergency' of plastics littering seas and oceans," lamenting the lack of protection of the God-given gift of the "great waters and all they contain." He exclaims, "We cannot allow our seas and oceans to be littered by endless fields of floating plastic" (https://www.nbcnews.com/news/world/pope-francis-urges-action-endless-fields-plastic-world-s-oceans-n905711). Explore and discuss concrete changes that can be made in your homes, parishes, schools, institutions, and businesses to help address this emergency. Reflect on the ritual of grace before meals. What or who are you appreciating? What are your thankful for? How do your purchases reflect your care of creation and the gift of water in your life? How could grace before meals help inspire new, just behaviors?

INTERACTIVE ACTIVITIES AND DISCUSSION QUESTIONS FOR CHAPTERS 4–6

WHAT DO YOU KNOW ABOUT EARTH?

Instructions: Sign up for a free quizlet account at https://quizlet.com. Search for the quizlet titled "What Do You Know about Earth" by WU religion alumni C.J. James (cjjames1). Then take the following quiz to see how earth literate you are. You can choose from eight different ways to interact with the materials. Take a test to see what you know or use flashcards to learn more or really test yourself via the timed matching game. Afterward, reflect individually or as a group on the following questions:

1. Was there anything that surprised you? How literate do you feel about Earth?
2. What about Earth's landscapes and inspirited bodies could you celebrate more? Are there any aspects that concern you?
3. How could this knowledge impact how you appreciate and use soil, people, or places in your everyday life and in your faith life?

CHAPTERS 4–6 REFLECTION AND DISCUSSION QUESTIONS

1. Spend some time praying in nature where you have found solitude and serenity. Bring with you the following passage from *Laudato Si'*: "The entire material universe speaks of God's love, his boundless affection for us....The history of our friendship with God is always linked to particular places which take on an intensely personal meaning....Anyone who has grown up on the hills or used to sit by the spring to drink or played out-

doors in the neighborhood square; going back to these places is a chance to recover something of their true selves" (*LS* 84). Go to your chosen space. For a moment, close your eyes. Take a deep breath. Breathe in. Pause for a second. And now breathe out. Notice how you are sitting. Is your body relaxed or tense? Breathe in and think *peace*. Then breathe out and think *joy*. Notice your breath—then clear your mind of thoughts. Start to get acquainted with your space—what do you hear? Smell? Open your eyes and look around you. What colors, textures, and beauty do you see? What is the smallest detail you notice? Biggest? How does this ecosystem and its many residents communicate the divine? What does this particular communion of God's beloved subjects need for abundant life? What can you do (or avoid doing) to help achieve this?

2. Take some time to reflect on the biblical artwork of Nathan Greene, especially *Ever Interceding*. This portrait captures the angst Jesus felt in the garden of Gethsemane and yet it is set in a cosmic, planetary context. How could this artwork speak to the challenges facing Earth outlined in chapter 4? What parts of the biblical narrative in the garden could lead us to hope and not despair today? Take a moment to connect this artwork with the video "Reclaiming Jesus" (Christian Methodist Episcopal Churches): https://www.youtube.com/watch?v=KpmjurAXAok. Discuss its strengths and weaknesses.
3. Read the following taken from Diana Butler Bass's text *Grounded* (2017):

> The table reminds us that the centre of our lives is a feast in which we celebrate the gifts of food and community, and remember our ancestors and the Giver. The habits we bring to the table can make or break the party. (183)
>
> Instead of thinking of Revelation's sacred city as a sort of imperial throne room, perhaps we should see it as a dining room. And around the table are many chairs. The places are marked with the cards: "Christian," "Jew," "Muslim," "Buddhist," "American," "Arab," "Chinese," "African," "Human," "Animal," "Fish," "Tree," and so on. No one owns the table. No one gets to take it over. We receive this table; it is the gift of heaven to earth. Our job is to pull up more chairs. And make sure all are fed. Where is God? God hosts the table at the center of the world. The sacred cosmos is a feast, a party of host and guests, seated around the table that practices hospitality for all. (272).

How are you making or breaking the party? How could you "pull up" more chairs to the tables you sit at? What needs to be done to enact this vision of cosmic hospitality and the messianic banquet in churches and communities in the United States?

4. After reflecting on chapter 6, watch the following video created by the United Way of the Carolinas in 2015: https://www.youtube.com/watch?v=rTelylW1bOY. This video shows that where you live strongly impacts how well off your kids will be. How can Christian churches work to address this "zip code" injustice? Could urban "agrihoods" be part of the solution? Explore Michigan's Urban Farming Initiative at https://www.youtube.com/watch?time_continue=3&v=f8ErRNiHBAM and then discuss concrete ways (e.g., land use, volunteers, donations, leadership) your parish, communities, and families can address social, economic, and ecological injustice.
5. Wendell Berry inspires readers to be forest Christians:

   > I used the phrase "forest Christian" to suggest what has been, for me, a necessary shift in perspective on the New Testament: from that of the church to that of the whole Creation....I feel more and more strongly that when St. Paul said that "we are members of one another," he was using a far more inclusive "we" than Christian institutions have generally thought. For me, this is the meaning of ecology. Whether we know it or not, whether we want to be or not, we are members of one another: humans (ourselves and our enemies), earthworms, whales, snakes, squirrels, trees, topsoil, flowers, weeds, germs, hills, rivers, swifts, and stones—all of 'us.'"[1]

   How does this echo the idea of integral ecology and spirituality in *Laudato Si'*? In what concrete ways can you cultivate a deeper love for your leafy neighbors?
6. Watch the short video by mycologist Paul Stamets called "Fantastic Fungi: The Spirit of Good" at https://www.youtube.com/watch?v=2wzBPSbTGYM. What was your initial reaction? How did this film help you to see how fungi are our special neighbors in our common home? How could this inform your Christian imaginations and acts of faith?
7. *Laudato Si'* inspires our theological imaginations to embrace our identity as part of a communion of inspired bodies. How can your church and family bring this incarnational truth more alive at Christmas? Meditate on Luke 2:8–14 and then read the thoughts of environmentalist Stephen Scharper (https://www.thestar.com/opinion/contributors/2017/12/24/charlie-brown-and-the-quandary-of-christmas.html). How could we witness to these angelic glad tidings in "ordinary" moments of our lives (e.g., preparing meals, baby showers, weddings, and burials)? The following resources can help continue the conversation: Serlo Education, "Keeping Pet Worms," https://youtu.be/SCJ7nzKwnYo; *Evolving Motherhood*, "How to Throw an Earth Friendly Baby Shower," http://evolvingmotherhood.com/2011/06/how-to-throw-an-earth-friendly-baby-shower.html; Good Morning

America, "Earth Day Weddings," https://www.goodmorningamerica.com/living/story/earth-day-weddings-eco-friendly-couples-share-green-54292843; Green Burial Council, "FAQs: Green Burial Defined," https://www.greenburialcouncil.org/green_burial_defined.html; Treehugger, "Egg-Shaped Burial Pods Feed the Trees and Turn Cemeteries into Forests," https://www.treehugger.com/culture/egg-shaped-burial-pods-fertilize-forest.html.

8. Take some time to watch one or more of these films: *Evan Almighty* (2007), *Avatar* (2009), *The Lorax* (2012), *Zootopia* (2016). Discuss what helped to change destructive attitudes, values, and behaviors toward places and peoples, so that individuals and communities found reconciliation, ecological and social justice, and peace. Not unlike these films, how does *Laudato Si'* carefully balance distress and hope? Discuss why it is important to keep hope in a creative tension with distress—especially as Christians.
9. Explore the Dominican Sisters' commitment to right relationship to the land, creation care spirituality, and ecotheological education at the Genesis Farm in New Jersey (http://genesisfarm.org/about/16) and their house of formation in California (https://www.vmwp.com/projects/dominican-sisters-house-of-formation/). What creation care message does your church building teach? How could that message be changed? What steps can you take in your own homes and schools to ensure creation care catechesis is being done in word, deed, and structure?
10. Meditate on the powerful ideas in paragraphs 84–92 in *Laudato Si'* and then contemplate the following passage from Robert Moor's book *On Trails* (2016):

    When I was younger I used to see the earth as a fundamentally stable and serene place....Now I see the earth as the collaborative artwork of trillions of sculptors, large and small. Sheep, humans, elephants, ants: each of us alters the world in our passage. When we build hives or nests, mud huts or concrete towers, we re-sculpt the contours of the planet. When we eat, we convert living matter into waste. And when we walk, we create trails. The question we must ask ourselves is not whether we should shape the earth but how. (130–31)

    How do both authors appreciate the value of Earth's many inspirited bodies? What can your parish do to cultivate the different sense of "place" offered by *Laudato Si'* and reshape the path humans are creating on Earth?

INTERACTIVE ACTIVITIES AND DISCUSSION QUESTIONS FOR CHAPTERS 7–9

WHAT DO YOU KNOW ABOUT AIR?

Instructions: Sign up for a free quizlet account at https://quizlet.com. Search for the quizlet titled "What Do You Know about Air" by WU religion alumni C.J. James (cjjames1). Then take the following quiz to see how water literate you are. You can choose from eight different ways to interact with the materials. Take a test to see what you know or use flashcards to learn more or really test yourself via the timed matching game. Afterward, reflect individually or as a group on the following questions:

1. Was there anything that surprised you? How literate do you feel about Earth's atmosphere?
2. What about air and avian neighbors could you celebrate more? Are there any aspects that concern you?
3. How could this knowledge impact how you appreciate air in your everyday life and in your faith life?

CHAPTERS 7–9 REFLECTION AND DISCUSSION QUESTIONS

1. Check out your Air Quality Index over several days or even months at https://airnow.gov/. How good was the air that you breathed in? Look at areas with moderate to unhealthy levels of air quality. Discuss the vision of justice and peace offered by Scripture and *Laudato Si'* in light of this knowledge. Then watch Rob Bell's "Breathe" (https://www

.youtube.com/watch?v=-EFLRDNAx-Y). Explore how his understanding of God's breath and our breath changes when air is not purifying and not life-giving. Discuss ways you and your faith community can contribute to cleaner air at https://airnow.gov/index.cfm?action=resources .whatyoucando.

2. Read the following passage by Stephen Bede Scharper in *For Earth's Sake* (Novalis, 2013), 173–74:

   > Did you ever think of giving up your car? When I posed this question to my wife several years ago, she rolled her eyes....I felt like Galileo proposing a heliocentric universe to Pope Urban VIII. Suddenly I was questioning a sacred tradition....Perhaps we might view striving for societal sustainability as not just a matter of sacrifice. This isn't about everyone giving up one's car; it is about discerning how we are to relate to this new ecological moment. Sometimes fundamental changes make room in your life for new and fine things to happen. It's not just about sacrifice, but about making a space for a novel and possibly enhanced way of life. It may also hold hidden harvests for the spiritual and materials well-being, not only of our families and nation, but of our larger household, the Earth.

   Would you give up your car? How would your life change? What hidden harvests could there be?

3. Watch the following TED Talk entitled, "Why We Shouldn't Trust Our Markets with Our Civic Life" by Michael Sandel: https://www.ted.com/talks/michael_sandel_why_we_shouldn_t_trust_markets_with_our_civic_life. What surprised you? Concerned you? What questions arose for you after watching this TED Talk? In what ways (systems of education, housing, etc.) are we disconnected from those who differ from us (class, ethnicity, age)? How is this segregation inhibiting our democracy and diminishing our spiritual identities and images of a relational God?
4. Photosynthesis is the process by which green plants take in carbon dioxide and release oxygen into the atmosphere. Watch the "Earth 'Breathing'" video created by NASA and NOAA Scientists at https://www.youtube.com/watch?v=hrl0zqUNdlg. What questions or concerns do you have? What aspects of your faith tradition could speak to what is happening to Earth's atmosphere and climate?
5. Listen to Kim Walker-Smith's "Holy Spirit" (https://www.youtube.com/watch?time_continue=2&v=eFByOX8Fb0M) or "Spirit Move" by Kalley Heiligenthal (https://www.youtube.com/watch?v=tbdSQ8MLnYs). Then explore your favorite hymns and Christian worship music about the Holy Spirit.

How do they describe or visualize the Spirit's presence in the world? How do they describe the Spirit's power at work in the world? How could this understanding of the Spirit move us to protect our air?

6. The avian death toll due to light pollution and glass buildings is second only to habitat destruction. Read the following *Washington Post* article (2013) about our avian neighbors: https://www.washingtonpost.com/local/how-many-birds-die-from-hitting-dc-buildings-volunteers-are-trying-to-find-out/2013/10/14/60aaca06-344c-11e3-8a0e-4e2cf80831fc_story.htm. What are some of the things being done to address what is happening to these neighbors of ours? Explore other ways to help at Mass Audobon (https://www.massaudubon.org/learn/nature-wildlife/birds/bird-window-collisions) and American Bird Conservancy (https://abcbirds.org/wp-content/uploads/2015/04/Bird-friendly_Building_Guide_WEB.pdf). What ways could you or your church be more proactive about protecting our avian neighbors?
7. Environmental Health Centers based at the University of Southern California are empowering youths to track air pollution in their areas and become more directly involved with environmental justice issues affecting their communities. Explore the educational and potential faith dimensions of the article, "Youth Pollution Monitoring Activities across the Southland," at https://envhealthcenters.usc.edu/2014/07/youth-pollution-monitoring-activities-across-the-southland.html. How does their approach to justice speak to the working of the Holy Spirit in our world today? How can your church or community empower youths to be stewards and protectors of the world they will be inheriting?

INTERACTIVE ACTIVITIES AND DISCUSSION QUESTIONS FOR CHAPTERS 10–12

WHAT DO YOU KNOW ABOUT FIRE?

Instructions: Sign up for a free quizlet account at https://quizlet.com. Search for the quizlet titled "What Do You Know about Fire" by WU religion alumni C.J. James (cjjames1). Then take the following quiz to see how water literate you are. You can choose from eight different ways to interact with the materials. Take a test to see what you know or use flashcards to learn more or really test yourself via the timed matching game. Afterward, reflect individually or as a group on the following questions:

1. Was there anything that surprised you? How literate do you feel about fire and energy?
2. What about fire, climate, or energy could you celebrate more? Are there any aspects that concern you?
3. How could this knowledge impact how you appreciate energy in your everyday life and in your faith life?

CHAPTERS 10–12 REFLECTION AND DISCUSSION QUESTIONS

1. Catholic Climate Covenant originated in 2006 to implement Catholic social teaching on ecology within the U.S. church. This group offers many resources for parishes to learn more about changes in our atmosphere and faithful responses being made at all levels of the Catholic Church. One great resource is "Homily Helps": Look at the "Homily Help" for the 17th Sunday of Ordinary Time, Cycle B (https://

catholicclimatecovenant.org/files/resource/attachment/IntegralFaith-OrdinaryTimeB2c17thSundayJuly29.pdf). What did you like about the messages and highlights offered? How could this help cultivate a more robust Christian spirituality? Feel free to check out other Sundays.

2. Watch "The Story of Stuff" (2007) at https://storyofstuff.org/movies/story-of-stuff/. Discuss how you, your family, or your church could be more authentic energy stewards?
3. Explore the pros and cons of the following renewable energies: wind, solar, geothermal, and hydropower. Here are some good sites to get the conversation started: EIA, "Renewable Energy Explained," https://www.eia.gov/energyexplained/?page=renewable_home; Sunpower, "A Complete Guide to 7 Renewable Energy Sources," https://us.sunpower.com/complete-guide-7-renewable-energy-sources. How could your homes, schools, businesses, and churches embrace renewable energies?
4. Reflect on the Scripture passage Matthew 22:37–40. Discuss the idea of who are our neighbors in the twenty-first century and how we are called to care for them. After starting this discussion, watch the following video from Catholic Climate Covenant (Feast of St. Francis 2018) at https://www.youtube.com/watch?v=oyjHVxilh6E. How did these ideas change or augment your discussions? What has now become more challenging?
5. The organization 350.org was founded in part by environmentalist Bill McKibben (*The Comforting Whirlwind: God, Job, and the Scale of Creation*, Cowley, 2005) in 2008, and it is a global grassroots climate movement holding political, social, and spiritual leaders accountable to science and justice. Its name is derived from 350 parts per million—the safe concentration of CO_2 in the atmosphere. Watch "Climate Change Is about Power" (https://www.youtube.com/watch?v=m95K7LCIlC4). What echoed what was written in *Laudato Si'*? How could a focus on the triune family help people of faith make sense of what was presented by 350.org? How can your family or church be a part of this grassroots movement?
6. Have participants check out package-free shopping: https://packagefreeshop.com. As you explore the package-free mission, services, and products, ask yourself the following questions: What products do you buy now that could be package free? Why are they packaged? What products must be packaged? What is the predominant material used for packaging? Are there other options if an item must be packaged?

NOTES

PREFACE

1. "Biography of the Holy Father Francis," http://w2.vatican.va/content/francesco/en/biography/documents/papa-francesco-biografia-bergoglio.html.

2. For example, his denunciation of pope and priest worship (clericalism), his use of public transit, his embrace of recovering addicts and those with disabilities, his encouragement of youths, and his attention to ecological interests.

3. Pope Francis, *Laudato Si'* (Washington, DC: USCCB, 2015), no. 14. Later references will be abbreviated *LS*, followed by the paragraph number.

INTRODUCTION

1. Catherine Wright, *Creation, God, and Humanity: Engaging the Mystery of Suffering within the Sacred Cosmos* (Mahwah, NJ: Paulist Press, 2017).

2. Erin Lothes Biviano, "Elizabeth Johnson and Cantors of the Universe," in *Turning to the Heavens and the Earth: Theological Reflections on a Cosmological Conversion*, ed. Julia Brumbaugh and Natalia Imperatori-Lee (Collegeville, MN: Liturgical Press, 2016), 185.

3. Stephen B. Scharper, *For Earth's Sake: Toward a Compassionate Ecology*, ed. Simon Appolloni (Toronto: Novalis, 2013), 193.

PART I: INTRODUCTION

1. Rachel Carson and Linda Lear, "Lost Woods: The Discovered Writing of Rachel Carson," Publicism, 1999, http://publicism.info/environment/woods/12.html.

2. In September 2000, world leaders came together to adopt a set of Millennium Development Goals (MDGs) to address serious issues facing all humans living on this Blue Marble. One goal was reducing the number of people, by half the proportion, who lack

access to improved sources of water by 2015. After a concerted, international effort, this target was met, but many others associated with water were not. This inspired seventeen new Sustainable Development Goals (SDGs)—several of which revolve around water. Goal 6 calls for clean water and sanitation, Goal 3 calls for good health and well-being—impossible without water; Goals 14 and 15 are concerned about aquatic and terrestrial life respectively, both of which are dependent on water; Goal 12 calls for responsible consumption and production, which involves water, and Goal 16 calls for peace—something impossible without access to water.

3. Orr writes, "The result [of a malformed consciousness] is a generation of ecological yahoos without a clue why the color of the water in their rivers is related to their food supply, or why storms are becoming more severe as the planet warms. The same persons as adults will create businesses, vote, have families, and above all, consume. If they come to reflect on the discrepancy between the splendor of their private lives in a hotter, more toxic and violent world, as ecological illiterates they will have roughly the same success as one trying to balance a check-book without knowing arithmetic." David. W Orr, *Ecological Literacy: Education and the Transition to a Postmodern World* (Albany: State University of New York Press, 1992).

CHAPTER 1

1. Quote from Pontifical Council for Justice and Peace, *LS* 106.

2. It is only 32 percent but it is the largest contributor to water being unavailable because it has evaporated, transpired, been incorporated into products or crops, consumed by humans or livestock, or otherwise removed from the immediate water environment. Agricultural irrigation consumed 85 percent of the total water withdrawn in the United States in 2003, and in 2012 the figure lies between 80 and 90 percent. From P. Torcellini, N. Long, and R. Judkoff, "Consumptive Water Use for U.S. Power Production," *Technical Report* (Colorado: National Renewable Energy Laboratory, 2003), 8, https://www.nrel.gov/docs/fy04osti/33905.pdf; Molly A. Maupin et al., "Estimated Use of Water in the United States in 2010," Circular 1405, U.S. Geological Survey, n.d., 29, https://pubs.usgs.gov/circ/1405/pdf/circ1405.pdf.

3. Other energy procurement methods (mining for petroleum; hydroelectric power plants) also consume water but to lesser degrees than thermoelectric. From Maupin et al., "Estimated Use of Water in the United States in 2010."

4. Energy Waste report from Lisa Zyga, "US Energy Use Chart Shows We Waste More Than Half of Our Energy," Phys.org, April 9, 2011, https://phys.org/news/2011-04-energy_1.html; Energy conservation report from "Energy Saver: Tips on Saving Money and Energy at Home" (U.S. Department of Energy, May 2014), DOE/GO-102014-4405, https://www.energy.gov/sites/prod/files/2014/09/f18/61628_BK_EERE-EnergySavers_w150.pdf.

5. “Product Gallery,” Water Footprint Network, 2017, http://waterfootprint.org/en/resources/interactive-tools/product-gallery/.

6. U.S. Environmental Protection Agency, “Advancing Sustainable Materials Management: 2014 Fact Sheet,” November 2016, EPA530-R-17-01, https://www.epa.gov/sites/production/files/2016-11/documents/2014_smmfactsheet_508.pdf.

7. U.S. Environmental Protection Agency, 7.

8. UNESCO and Environmental Working Group, “Imperfect: Ugly Produce Delivery for 30–50% Less,” Imperfect Produce, https://www.imperfectproduce.com/.

9. Pope Benedict XVI: “Purchasing is always a moral—and not simply economic—act,” and every penny spent indicates what and who we value as Christians and institutions (quoted in *LS* 206).

10. U.S. Environmental Protection Agency, “Statistics and Facts,” Overviews and Factsheets, U.S. EPA, January 23, 2017, https://www.epa.gov/watersense/statistics-and-facts.

11. See part 4, “Fire,” for more information.

12. Trevor Nance, “Idyllic Caribbean Island Covered in a Tide of Plastic Trash along Coastline,” *Forbes*, October 27, 2017, https://www.forbes.com/sites/trevornace/2017/10/27/idyllic-caribbean-island-covered-in-a-tide-of-plastic-trash-along-coastline/#683081372524.

13. Claire Le Guern, “When the Mermaids Cry: The Great Plastic Tide,” *Coastal Care*, 2017, http://plastic-pollution.org/.

14. Thankfully, legislative steps have been taken and by July 1, 2018 rinse-off cosmetics and nonprescription drugs will be microbead free, and many places are going plastic bag free (or charging a fee). From FDA, “The Microbead-Free Waters Act: FAQs,” WebContent, U.S. Food & Drug Administration, November 3, 2017, https://www.fda.gov/Cosmetics/GuidanceRegulation/LawsRegulations/ucm531849.htm.

15. Ellen MacArthur Foundation, “A New Textiles Economy: Redesigning Fashion’s Future,” 2017, https://www.ellenmacarthurfoundation.org/publications.

16. Chris Tyree and Dan Morrison, “Invisibles: The Plastic Inside Us,” Online Journalism Organization, Orb Media, http://orbmedia.org/stories/Invisibles_plastics/.

17. Dr. Sherri Mason of the State University of New York at Fredonia and Elizabeth Wattenberg at the University of Minnesota, School of Public Health conducted a study where tap water from all over the world was tested, and they found that over 80 percent of the samples had microplastics present. This information was funded and released by Orb Media, a DC-based nonprofit digital newsroom, in Tyree and Morrison, “Invisibles: The Plastic Inside Us.”

18. USGS Water Science School, “Rain and Precipitation,” United States Geological Survey, October 27, 2017, https://water.usgs.gov/edu/earthrain.html.

19. Mid-America Regional Council, “What Is Sediment Pollution?” https://cfpub.epa.gov/npstbx/files/ksmo_sediment.pdf.

20. “Top U.S. States by Number of Hogs and Pigs 2018,” Statista, https://www.statista.com/statistics/194371/top-10-us-states-by-number-of-hogs-and-pigs/.

21. "Coral Reefs Buffer Shorelines from Waves to Diminish Storm Damage, Provide Food and Recreation, and Can Also Supply New," n.d.

22. Michigan Civil Rights Commission, "Michigan Civil Rights Commission Report: Race and Racism Played Roles in Causing the Flint Water Crisis, and Both Blacks and Whites Are Victims," Report of the Michigan Civil Rights Commission, The Flint Water Crisis: Systematic Racism through the Lens of Flint, February 17, 2017, https://www.michigan.gov/mdcr/0,4613,7-138--405318--a,00.html.

CHAPTER 3

1. "Let All Creation Praise," http://www.letallcreationpraise.org/home; Creation Justice Ministries, http://www.creationjustice.org/; Earth Day Resources, "Water, Holy Water," 2014, https://salsa4.salsalabs.com/o/50750/images/Final%20Earth%20Day%202014%20CJM.pdf?key=95273412.

2. Interfaith Partners for the Environment, Green Faith, http://www.greenfaith.org/.

3. She noticed that the bacteria Streptomyces coelicolor makes a striking red-purple pigment, and now she's using it to develop bold, colorfast fabric dye that cuts down on water waste and chemical runoff, compared with traditional dyes. See Natsai Audrey Chieza, "Fashion Has a Pollution Problem—Can Biology Fix It?," https://www.ted.com/talks/natsai_audrey_chieza_fashion_has_a_pollution_problem_can_biology_fix_it.

4. Blood: Water, https://www.bloodwater.org/; "Mission Statement," Living Water International, https://water.cc/mission-statement.

5. For example, host water conservation Sundays, bulletin messages, science lessons infused with Christian spirituality (e.g., the Blue Marble as an interconnected communion; loggerhead turtles need protection from plastic waste because "each creature reflects something of God," *LS* 221); and participate in World Water Day—see "What Is World Water Day?," World Water Day, 2018, http://worldwaterday.org/.

6. Lisa Tabachnick, "Federation of the Sisters of St. Joseph of Canada Becomes a Blue Community: Working towards Making Clean Water a Human Right," Sisters of St. Joseph of Toronto, December 7, 2017, http://www.csj-to.ca/story/2017/12/federation-sisters-st-joseph-canada-becomes-blue-community-working-towards-making-clea.

7. Sisters of Mercy are also outspoken advocates: "We choose to recommit ourselves to care for Earth, attending to the issues of climate change, the human right to clean water, and the dangers of extractive industries." "Word of Comfort to our Suffering World" (Action Alert April 2, 2018) from Barbara Turnbull, "58 Elderly Nuns Move into Their Final Home on Earth," *The Star*, March 15, 2013, https://www.thestar.com/life/2013/03/15/58_elderly_nuns_find_a_tiny_piece_of_heaven_on_earth.html. The Society of Jesus, or Jesuits, have also done much to address water poverty at an international level. A global, earth-centered network of Jesuits and other partners (the Ecojesuits) were present at the COP23, and provide resources to connect water issues and Catholic Social Teaching in response to *Laudato Si'*. Jesuit European Social Centre, "Ecojesuit at COP23," Jesuit European Social Cen-

tre, November 1, 2017, http://jesc.eu/ecojesuit-at-cop23/; Frank Turner, "Water in Catholic Social Teaching," Ecology and Jesuits in Communication, EcoJesuit, http://www.ecojesuit.com/water-in-catholic-social-teaching/5691/; see *LS* 162.

8. Minnesota Catholic Conference, "November 2: Care for Creation," 2016, https://vimeo.com/187861340.

9. John Bullas, "Spirited Reflection: Living Water," KAIROS Canada, March 14, 2017, https://www.kairoscanada.org/living-water.

10. "Water CRS Education," Catholic Relief Services, https://education.crs.org/issus/water.

11. For example, in 2017 Bears Ears National Monument was diminished from 1.35 million acres to 201,876 acres—an 85 percent decrease—and at the same time the Grand Staircase-Escalante National Monument was also diminished 45 percent.

PART II: INTRODUCTION

1. Fred Bahnson and Norman Wirzba, *Making Peace with the Land: God's Call to Reconcile with Creation*, Resources for Reconciliation (Westmont, IL: IVP Books, 2012), 102.

CHAPTER 4

1. John Feehan, *The Singing Heart of the World: Creation, Evolution, and Faith* (Maryknoll, NY: Orbis Books, 2012), 62, 66.

2. World Wildlife Fund, "Living Planet Report 2016," https://www.worldwildlife.org/pages/living-planet-report-2016.

3. Global Assessment Report on Biodiversity and Ecosystem Services (May 6, 2019) at www.un.org.

4. For a list of five major contributing factors to loss of biodiversity, see WWF, "Living Planet Report 2016."

5. "Major Depression," National Institute of Mental Health, https://www.nimh.nih.gov/health/statistics/major-depression.shtml.

6. "Homelessness Statistics by State," United States Interagency Council on Homelessness, https://www.usich.gov/tools-for-action/map/#fn[]=1500&fn[]=2900&fn[]=6100&fn[]=10100&fn[]=14100.

7. "Hotline Statistics," National Human Trafficking Hotline, https://humantraffickinghotline.org/states.

8. Peter Wagner and Wendy Sawyer, "Mass Incarceration: The Whole Pie 2018," Prison Policy Initiative, https://www.prisonpolicy.org/reports/pie2018.html.

9. Assistant Secretary of Public Affairs (ASPA), "What Is the U.S. Opioid Epidemic?," U.S. Department of Health and Human Services, December 4, 2017, https://www.hhs.gov/opioids/about-the-epidemic/index.html.

10. *LS* 47; Craig Chalquist, "A Look at Ecotherapy Research Evidence," *Ecopsychology* 1, no. 2 (June 2009): 1–11.

11. To figure out this percentage: **Income ÷ poverty guideline for household size = percentage of poverty guideline.** From "Food Security Status of U.S. Households in 2016," United States Department of Agriculture Economic Research Service, October 4, 2017, https://www.ers.usda.gov/topics/food-nutrition-assistance/food-security-in-the-us/key-statistics-graphics.aspx.

12. Food Research and Action Center, "How Hungry Is America?," FRAC's National, State, and Local Index of Food Hardship, June 2016, http://frac.org/wp-content/uploads/food-hardship-2016-1.pdf.

13. Diana Butler Bass, *Grounded: Finding God in the World—a Spiritual Revolution* (San Francisco: HarperOne, 2015).

14. 1.5 million North Carolinians are members of the Southern Baptist Convention, representing a third of all religious adherents in the state. The United Methodist Church has the second largest number of adherents statewide (659,000), followed by nondenominational Christian (565,000), Catholic (393,000), and Presbyterian (186,000). The African Methodist Episcopal (AME) Zion Church is the only other denomination with more than 100,000 adherents in North Carolina. From Rebecca Tippett, "Religion in North Carolina: Southern Baptists Dominate, Catholicism and Non-denominational Affiliation Rising," *Carolina Demography* (blog), June 2, 2014, https://demography.cpc.unc.edu/2014/06/02/religion-in-north-carolina-southern-baptists-dominate-catholicism-and-non-denominational-affiliation-rising/.

CHAPTER 6

1. Shonil A. Bhagwat, Nigel Dudley, and Stuart R. Harrop, "Religious Following in Biodiversity Hotspots: Challenges and Opportunities for Conservation and Development," *Conservation Letters* 4, no. 3 (June–July 2011): 234–40, https://doi.org/10.1111/j.1755-263X.2011.00169.x.

2. Cynthia Gibbs, "St. Eugene Parish 'Goes Green,'" *Catholic News Herald*, June 6, 2018, http://www.catholicnewsherald.com/90-news/local/3150-st-eugene-parish-goes-green.

3. Fred Bahnson recounts a story in *Soil and Sacrament* (New York: Simon & Schuster, 2013) of how this garden fed a neighbor (she stole watermelons to help offset her rent) but also planted seeds of hospitality that allowed this woman to participate in the life of the community more fully.

4. The Conservation Fund, "Faith and Food," https://www.conservationfund.org/projects/faith-and-food.

5. This ministry offers many innovative and inspiring activities, programming, and opportunities. For pastors especially, check out the Sabbath Life ministry—an ecumenical invitation to pastors and ministry professionals to embody a way of life grounded in

the practice of Sabbath. This is done via work in the garden, worship, holy communion, eating together faithfully, shared silence and rest, reflection together, and prayer. See Life Around the Table, http://lifearoundthetable.org/.

6. "Food That LAUGHS," *Life Around the Table* (blog), http://lifearoundthetable.org/about/food-that-laughs/.

7. They then gather solutions from around the world that are solving hunger problems and disseminate them to our active network. From "Core Values & History," ECHO, https://www.echonet.org/core-values-history/.

CHAPTER 7

1. NASA Climate Kids, "10 Interesting Things About Air," https://climatekids.nasa.gov/10-things-air/.

2. Alyssa Contreras, "Breathing Ancient Air," *Magazines at Marquette* (blog), February 14, 2017, https://medium.com/magazines-at-marquette/is-it-true-that-were-breathing-the-same-molecules-once-breathed-by-the-dinosaurs-julius-caesar-or-decaf242fe8b.

3. U.S. Environmental Protection Agency, "Criteria Air Pollutants," Policies and Guidance, U.S. EPA, April 9, 2014, https://www.epa.gov/criteria-air-pollutants.

4. "Air Quality Index (AQI) Basics," Air Now, https://airnow.gov/index.cfm?action=aqibasics.aqi.

5. "Key Findings: The State of the Air 2018," American Lung Association, http://www.lung.org/our-initiatives/healthy-air/sota/key-findings/.

6. "Key Findings: The State of the Air 2018."

7. "Health Effects of Ozone and Particle Pollution," American Lung Association, http://www.lung.org/our-initiatives/healthy-air/sota/health-risks/.

8. Sarah Gibbens, "Air Pollution Robs Us of Our Smarts and Our Lungs," *National Geographic*, August 31, 2018, https://www.nationalgeographic.com/environment/2018/09/news-air-quality-brain-cognitive-function/.

9. "Disparities in the Impact of Air Pollution," American Lung Association, http://www.lung.org/our-initiatives/healthy-air/outdoor/air-pollution/disparities.html.

10. Kenneth Qin, "Birds Suffer from Air Pollution, Just Like We Do," Audubon California, July 23, 2015, http://ca.audubon.org/news/birds-suffer-air-pollution-just-we-do.

11. Scott R. Loss et al., "Bird-Building Collisions in the United States: Estimates of Annual Mortality and Species Vulnerability—the Condor," *The Condor: Ornithological Applications*, January 2, 2014, 8–23.

12. U.S. Environmental Protection Agency, "EPA Takes Final Step in Phaseout of Leaded Gasoline," Reports and Assessments, U.S. Environmental Protection Agency, January 29, 1996, https://archive.epa.gov/epa/aboutepa/epa-takes-final-step-phaseout-leaded-gasoline.html.

13. Coral Davenport, "E.P.A. Takes a Major Step to Roll Back Clean Car Rules," *New York Times*, May 31, 2018, https://www.nytimes.com/2018/05/31/climate/epa-car-pollution-rollback.html.

CHAPTER 9

1. "Forest-Burning Is a Sin, Says Indonesian Fatwa. Story Reported around the World," Alliance of Religions and Conservation, September 15, 2016, http://www.arcworld.org/news.asp?pageID=821.

2. Molly Rauch, "Faith Leaders Call for Limits on Carbon Pollution," Moms Clean Air Force, February 26, 2014, https://www.momscleanairforce.org/faith-carbon-pollution/.

3. "Clergy and Faith Leaders Deliver Letter to Secretary Zinke Opposing Rollback of BLM Methane Waste Standards," Interfaith Power and Light, April 23, 2018, https://www.interfaithpowerandlight.org/2018/04/clergy-and-faith-leaders-deliver-letter-to-secretary-zinke-opposing-rollback-of-blm-methane-waste-standards/.

4. "Clergy and Faith Leaders Deliver Letter to Secretary Zinke."

5. Cindy Wooden, "Pope Tells Young Jesuits to Be Courageous, Prayerful, Creative," *National Catholic Reporter, The Francis Chronicles* (blog), August 2, 2018, https://www.ncronline.org/news/vatican/francis-chronicles/pope-tells-young-jesuits-be-courageous-prayerful-creative.

PART IV: INTRODUCTION

1. There are other forms of energy like mechanical energy (e.g., moving turbine blades due to the wind), electrical energy (e.g., motion of particles through a wire), chemical energy (e.g., stored energy in food or fuel), or nuclear energy (e.g., energy stored at the center of atoms like uranium).

2. Christiana Z. Peppard et al., "What Powers Us? A Comparative Religious Ethics of Energy Sources, Power, and Privilege," *Journal of the Society of Christian Ethics* 36, no. 1 (2016): 3–25, https://doi.org/10.1353/sce.2016.0010.

3. Pontifical Congregation for Justice and Peace, Mario Toso, and Peter Turkson, *Energy, Justice, and Peace: A Reflection on Energy in the Current Context of Development and Environmental Protection* (Mahwah, NJ: Paulist Press, 2016).

CHAPTER 10

1. "How Much Fuel Does an International Plane Use for a Trip?," How Stuff Works, https://science.howstuffworks.com/transport/flight/modern/question192.htm.

2. "What Is U.S. Electricity Generation by Energy Source?" U.S. Energy Information Administration, https://www.eia.gov/tools/faqs/faq.php?id=427&t=3.

3. Michael Hendryx and Benjamin Holland, "Unintended Consequences of the Clean Air Act: Mortality Rates in Appalachian Coal Mining Communities," *Environmental Science and Policy* 63 (September 2016): 1–6.

4. Natural gas is thought to be "cleaner" since it produces less carbon dioxide than coal, but when the extraction methods and harm done to those who live beside extraction points are considered, the human and ecosystemic costs of this energy are still too high and it too is not a life-giving option.

5. Abha Paraiulee and Frank Wania, "Evaluating Officially Reported Polycyclic Aromatic Hydrocarbon Emissions in the Athabasca Oil Sands Region with a Multimedia Fate Model," *Proceedings of the National Academy of Science of the United States of America* 111, no. 9 (March 4, 2014): 3344–49.

6. Beck was Administrator of EPA Region 2, 1977–79. Eckardt C. Beck, "The Love Canal Tragedy," *EPA Journal*, January 1979, https://archive.epa.gov/epa/aboutepa/love-canal-tragedy.html.

7. Christopher B. Field et al., "Summary for Policymakers," *Climate Change 2014: Impacts, Adaptation, and Vulnerability. Part A: Global and Sectoral Aspects. Contribution of Working Group II to the Fifth Assessment Report of the Intergovernmental Panel on Climate Change* (Cambridge University Press, 2014), https://www.ipcc.ch/pdf/assessment-report/ar5/wg2/ar5_wgII_spm_en.pdf.

CHAPTER 12

1. Elisabetta Povoledo, "Pope Tells Oil Executives to Act on Climate: 'There Is No Time to Lose,'" *New York Times*, June 9, 2018, https://www.nytimes.com/2018/06/09/world/europe/pope-oil-executives-climate-change.html.

2. Robin Gomes, "Pope Urges Sustainability, Just Distribution of Earth's Resources," *Vatican News*, Sept. 1, 2018, https://www.vaticannews.va/en/pope/news/2018-09/pope-francis-business-sustainability-development-care-creation.html.

3. Mark Oppenheimer, "Setting Aside a Scholarly Get-Together, for the Planet's Sake," *New York Times*, December 5, 2014, https://www.nytimes.com/2014/12/06/us/setting-aside-a-scholarly-get-together-for-the-planets-sake.html.

4. "2014 Preliminary Program Book," https://papers.aarweb.org/Preliminary_Program_Book_2014.pdf.

5. Some included the Jesuits in English Canada, the Diocese of the Holy Spirit of Umuarama in the Brazilian state of Paraná, SSM Health in the United States, and the Missionary Society of St. Columban.

6. Ed King, "Over 3000 UK Churches on Way to Ditching Fossil Fuels," *Climate Home News*, January 9, 2016, http://www.climatechangenews.com/2016/09/01/over-3000-uk-churches-on-way-to-ditching-fossil-fuels/.

7. Alanna Petroff, "Morocco: 15,000 Mosques Are Going Green," *CNN Tech*, November 15, 2016, https://money.cnn.com/2016/11/15/technology/morocco-energy-green-mosques/index.html.

8. Bishop Ellinah Wamukoya, "Green Anglicans—the Anglican Church of Southern Africa Votes to Divest from Fossil Fuels," Anglican Church of Southern African Environmental Network, Green Anglicans, http://www.greenanglicans.org/the-anglican-church-of-southern-africa-votes-to-divest-from-fossil-fuels/.

9. Fossil Free Funds, https://fossilfreefunds.org/.

10. As You Sow, https://www.asyousow.org/.

11. "Catholic Institutions Announce Fossil Fuel Divestment," the Global Catholic Climate Movement, October 4, 2016, https://catholicclimatemovement.global/release-catholic-institutions-announce-they-are-divesting-from-fossil-fuel-extraction/.

12. Gideon Weissman, "Renewables on the Rise 2018: A Decade of Progress toward a Clean Energy Future," Environment America Research & Policy Center (Frontier Group, July 2018), https://environmentamerica.org/sites/environment/files/reports/AME_Renewables-on-the-Rise_Jul18-Web.pdf.

13. Charles Fishman, *The Walmart Effect* (New York: Penguin Books, 2011).

14. Gideon Weissman, "Renewables on the Rise 2018."

15. United Church of Christ, "A Movement Is Born: Environmental Justice and the UCC," United Church of Christ, http://www.ucc.org/standing_rock_a_call_to_action.

16. Steven Martin, "NCC and Creation Justice Ministries Applaud Developments at Standing Rock," *National Council of Churches* (blog), December 5, 2016, http://nationalcouncilofchurches.us/ncc-and-creation-justice-ministries-applaud-developments-at-standing-rock/.

CHAPTERS 4–6 REFLECTION AND DISCUSSION QUESTIONS

1. Julia Brumbaugh and Natalia Imperatori-Lee, eds., *Turning to the Heavens and the Earth: Theological Reflections on a Cosmological Conversion; Essays in Honor of Elizabeth A. Johnson* (Collegeville, MN: Liturgical Press, 2016).